Long Lost Love
Diary of a Rambling Romeo

Michael Chapman Pincher

THE LILLIPUT PRESS

Advanced Reader Copy
To be published by
Lilliput Press
62-63 Arbour Hill
Dublin 7
Ireland

2024

Text © Michael Chapman Pincher
Maps & Cover © Mickeytwonames

ISBN 9781843518815

Back cover photo courtesy of Byron Newman

Contents

Maps

Dedication

I dedicate this book to the family that took me under their wing and let me sail with them on a once-in-a-lifetime journey. Even though it has been years, the memories are vivid. I look back fondly at the motley crew who allowed me to be part of their lives.

MCP March 2024

Introduction

Pirates, peccadillos, and picaresque pursuits in paradise

Long Lost Love is a nostalgic odyssey filled with unexpected twists, heartfelt moments, and engaging characters that transport you to another time and place. Every chapter has a palpable sense of wonder, a dash of whimsy and a double ration of home truths.

This book is a masterclass in plotting, pace, and character development. It's a thrilling ride from the start, full of unexpected twists that keep you guessing until the end.

'Michael makes writing look easy, and I know it's not.' - Simon Beaufoy, Screenwriter, *The Full Monty and Slumdog Millionaire*"

Preface

Long Lost Love is a self-contained book that draws inspiration from a journal detailing a voyage and the places and people encountered. It is a sequel to Long Lost Log: Diary of a Virgin Sailor, based on a rediscovered logbook returned to me forty-six years after I thought it lost forever.

Hoop is a twin-engine, 65-foot ketch-rigged motorsailer custom-built in the Lürssen shipyards on the Baltic coast of Germany. With his family on board, Count Camaris takes no chances as he navigates his precious cargo home to Canada.

Chapter I

Salted Wound

With mortal danger nipping at my heels, we set sail. Oblivious to my chequered past, Count Arno Camaris navigates *Hoop* into the Caribbean. As Puerto Rico disappears astern, I pump a clenched fist into the air with a sigh of relief. Yesterday, I was a dead man walking. Today, I'm a carefree deckhand embarking on my next adventure.

Hoop is a handsome vessel. Launched two years ago in 1973 to the count's specifications, she's now a storm-hardened, ocean-crossing wanderer—up to any challenge. As a robust twin-engine cruising yacht, her efficient, no-nonsense design makes the most of every inch of her 65-foot length, meaning we'll be living in close quarters.

Wafting up from the galley, I catch a whiff of sauerkraut. Despite the tropical heat, Anna, the count's capable wife, prepares a healthy lunch to feed her three daughters and two male crew. With seven on board there are always hungry mouths on board.

I'm almost through working out *Hoop*'s running gear as Eleven-year-old Mickie scampers up the deck with sprightly enthusiasm. We've not spoken yet, but if she's anything like her sisters, she'll have plenty to say and attitude with it.

'Hey, new crew. If you want me to show you the ropes, it'll cost you an ice cream when we arrive.'

'I'll bear that in mind.'

'Here's a joke for you: What did the captain's favourite daughter say to the deckhand?'

'No idea. What did she say?'

'If I wanted someone to admire the view, I'd have hired a tourist.' With juvenile vigour, she scrabbles up the ratlines. 'So long, sucker!'

'Foul winds and scurvy skies to you, too!' I shout aloft.

Mickie beams down with a mischievous grin. 'Gusty gales and galloping garfish with all the trimmings!'

The two other Camaris girls are as different as chalk and cheese. Nearly twenty, Lucie stands by her father, eager to raise the sails, while the quick-witted, work-shy Johanna is nowhere to be seen.

This is my third time lucky with the Camaris family. We first met in the Canary Islands while sailing across the Atlantic last year. Then, we crossed paths again in Antigua during a New Year's beach party in 1975. Fast-forward to yesterday when I spotted *Hoop* sail into San Juan harbour. Her massive Canadian flag and the hull's brooding silhouette were instantly recognizable. Shorthanded and eager to leave Puerto Rico, Count Camaris offered me a gig as a deckhand in exchange for a free ride to Vancouver, Canada. Given my circumstances, it was an offer I couldn't refuse. The only flaw in this maritime idyll is the first mate, Jerry. I found out in Antigua that he's a rogue. A former soldier and also British like me, he wouldn't be on board if he didn't have some ulterior motive.

***

I sway on the deck, the salty breeze stirring the familiar thrill of past adventures. It's hard to believe that a whole year has passed since I left England aboard the *Gay Gander*, a vessel bound for warmer waters. Under the watchful eye of John Farrell, the skipper and his stern mistress, Carola, I navigated through murky winter weather into clear blue Caribbean skies. But as that journey neared its end, I was cut adrift once more, dismissed without explanation. At twenty-two, with nothing but a rucksack and a well-thumbed copy of the *I Ching*, I faced a daunting choice: to persevere or scuttle back home in defeat.

That's where I first met Jerry—a Mr. Fix It—hustling among the wealthy yacht owners in English Harbour, Antigua. His offer of easy money and risky ventures tempted me, but my nerves failed me when push came to shove. Fleeing the fallout, I island-hopped up the Lesser Antilles until I found refuge in San Juan, Puerto Rico.

Broke and desperate, I hustled to survive in a world where opportunity and danger walked hand in hand. It was on those mean streets that I crossed paths with Ned, a San Juan pimp. He offered me a job paying me to escort the wives of high rollers so they could gamble without distraction. But our partnership soured when Ned's greed led to a fight that left him sprawled on the ground, either dead or unconscious. In the chaos, I snatched the pimp's ill-gotten gains hidden in his hatband, securing a wad of cash. Now, out to sea, one thing is sure, I am no longer a mere passenger but the captain of my destiny, ready to brave the waters—one wave at a time.

The presence of Jerry on board is awkward, though, as he knows about me. He's intent on raking up a past life I want to forget.

We're tidying away the mooring lines when he fixes me with his dead eyes. 'This friend of yours in Puerto Rico? The geezer who let you stay in his place. The one who's as queer as a two-dollar bill.'

'Yes, what about him?'

'You're telling me you didn't peddle your arse for rent?'

Getting no reply from me, he continues in his rough way. 'Good thing if you are a shirt lifter. Leaves the field open for me.' He nods towards Lucie and then Johanna, who has now come on deck and is lying prone and suntanned under the Caribbean sun. 'With luck, I'll shag them both.'

I guess he's using the gay tag as a way of gaining some advantage with the girls, neither of whom has deigned to notice either of us. They're well out of our league, sun-bleached blond, beautiful and blue-blooded, so unlikely to be interested in a pair of chancers picked up as flotsam along the way.

'Stop your nonsense,' I say, looking to where the two girls lie supine, their lithe, tanned bodies warming up under the morning sun. 'One's too classy, and the other's too innocent for you.'

'Stand by your bed, Saint Mick,' Jerry says, elbowing me in the ribs. 'The skipper's on his way.'

Count Arno Camaris strides down the deck, taller than us. His shoulders are squared, and his posture is impeccable, befitting a nobleman of the once-great Austro-Hungarian Empire.

Jerry defers to rank. 'We await your orders, Captain.'

'Good,' the count replies in his guttural accent, his mouth opening wide as he speaks. 'It'll be refreshing to have crew members who listen to me for once. The women on this boat tend to have their own ideas and opinions, especially Johanna!'

'Sounds like a recommendation to stay single,' quips Jerry. 'I was married to the army. Not sure I'm ready for another commitment.'

Arno laughs. 'Believe me, I understand. I'm looking forward to the end of this trip when my only companion will be my American Express Gold Card—a status symbol to match my new status.'

Jerry and I laugh in case we're supposed to.

'You think that is a joke?' Arno responds, pointing out that with an Austrian upbringing he says what he means and means what he says—no beating around the bush for our skipper.

Put on notice, Jerry and I stiffen to attention.

'How long until we reach the Canal?' I ask.

'Mit Glück, Mick, we should reach our destination in about ten days. Assuming good weather.' The count speaks English well, though his Germanic roots shine through.

'Then we go through the Canal and out in the Pacific for a thirty-day journey to Hawaii. We will spend some time cruising the islands before we go back to Canada. This will be a once-in-a-lifetime trip!'

'Can't wait,' I babble, excited as a child about Christmas.

'Trouble with sailing,' quips Jerry, 'you have no choice but to wait. You wait for the wind, the tide, orders and…'

'Sadly,' Arno interrupts, 'you both have to wait for breakfast. First mate, you're on the helm in ten minutes. Mick, wait for Anna and Lucie to show you how to hoist the topsail.'

He turns and marches back to *Hoop*'s large centre cockpit.

Jerry picks at the peeling varnish of the spruce mainmast. 'Wonder what he did during the war?'

'Probably in the Hitler Youth movement,' I say, figuring he was too young to fight.

Jerry mimics a Sieg Heil salute.

'Children had no choice.' I counter.

'Maybe I can claim those girls as a war prize,' Jerry suggests.

'Man, you're incorrigible.'

'Mind your language, you little poof. I've no idea what you mean.'

Jerry's joshing is tedious, but I try not to let it bring me down, and on hearing the Maple Leaf ensign snapping in the early-morning breeze, I shout out, 'Canada, here we come!'

'Don't get too excited, geezer,' Jerry says, showing his West London roots. 'It'll be the longest two months you'll ever remember. Boiling one end, freezing the other and dull as ditchwater in between.' Leaving me with his gloomy Eeyore sentiments, he works his way up the deck to take a turn at the helm.

My role on *Hoop* consists of hoisting and dropping sails, and although it's lubberly to refer to her as a cutter ketch, she has two headsails. With a complex but versatile rig, I've plenty of work aside from keeping watch and taking my stint at steering.

Waiting for Anna and Lucie, I gaze at the gunmetal sea as we head into the Mona Passage when a wave crashes over the bow. The salty spray stings my fresh wound. It's a stark reminder of my narrow escape when Ned attacked me with his swordstick. Lucky for me, one of his working girls warned me about his secret weapon, giving me the advantage when it came to blows to strike first. With a livid scar reminding me of the encounter, I'm relieved now, that here on the boat, there's nothing to worry about except breakfast.

Hoop plows into deeper waters, and the sounds of sailing fill the air: the rumble of rigging blocks losing tension, then snapping taut; the wind singing through the rigging; and the clunk of the rudder on its pintles as swells pass beneath. It's great to be back.

For a getaway boat, *Hoop* is hard to beat. She's steel-hulled with a raked wineglass stern and an elegant sheer line that rises towards a four-foot spruce bowsprit. The scratches and scrapes on the black-and-white paintwork—acquired during her maiden voyage from Europe—give character, while the spacious and sturdy design makes her vessel for a live-aboard family about to take on the Pacific Ocean.

We are heading towards the Isthmus of Darien, the thin sliver of land connecting the Americas, the geographic equivalent of Michelangelo's fingers of God and Adam on the ceiling of the Sistine Chapel. We sail on, and the Caribbean islands vanish from sight. Beneath my feet, I can feel the deck purring from the thrust of Dick and Harry—the nicknames of *Hoop*'s twin diesel engines—now propelling us south by southwest. Beneath the golden sun, the Spanish Main unfolds—an endless canvas of turquoise waters and azure sky. Sailing through these historic waters, where treasure-laden galleons once plundered the New World and pirates hunted for gold-filled holds, I think of on our cargo—a less glamorous collection of sauerkraut, sausages, and beans. Yet, amidst the seafaring legends of this treacherous passage, I hear echoes of the transatlantic slave trade that saw millions of enslaved Africans forcibly transported to replace the indigenous workforce ravaged by European diseases.

My daydream is short-lived when Mickie, agile as a monkey, clambers back down the ratlines. Similar to Scout in *To Kill a Mockingbird*, but with a blond pudding basin haircut, she treats the boat like a gymnasium and swings through the rigging as her mother and sister Lucie heave out a sailbag from the forehatch.

'This sail is called *Modder en Bloed*,' Anna says in a linguistic mix of her native Dutch and adopted Canadian, structural peculiarities I'll have to get used to.

'That's Mud and Blood to you,' Mickie explains. 'Unless you can speak lots of languages like me.'

'Is one of them double-Dutch?' I quip. She responds with a screwball face and a poke of the tongue.

When we unroll the topsail from its canvas bag, I grasp the reason for its name. The brown and ox-blood-striped canvas is the final part of the sail plan needed to harness as much of the warm easterly wind blowing across our beam as possible.

The light material flaps excitedly in the breeze, seemingly eager to fly puffed out and proud between the masts.

Jerry heads us into the wind. We haul the triangular cloth skyward into the space between the main and the mizzenmast.

'This will oomph us up,' Anna says, cobbling words together in her usual way. 'In bad weather, we drop the mainsail and use the jib and the jigger.'

With a kind face and no-nonsense attitude, Anna is at once likable. She has mothered, nursed, and fed her family since Arno's decision to take a sabbatical from working as a systems analyst in the growing world of computer science and bring them on an oceangoing, globetrotting odyssey. Physically strong and stubborn, she stands on the deck like a force of nature while Lucie, cut from the same cloth, teaches me how to trim the sails.

'Start trimming from the bow and work your way back,' she says, pointing out the jib's tell-tales, the guides to a sail's efficiency. Lucie's diligence is a warning—no wind will be wasted when she's in charge. 'Make sure the yarns on both sides of the canvas stream straight back. If the leeward one stops, head up to the wind, or fall off if the windward one hangs down.'

'What, like this?' I say, in a camp voice while showing her a limp wrist, before realizing it may send her the wrong signal. The gesture stops her in her tracks as though she sees me differently.

'I like you, Mick,' she says. 'I think we're going to get on. It will be good to have a friend to talk to.' Hearing a sound aloft, she peers up and catches Mickie who jumps down from the rigging. Together they scamper back to the cockpit to make sail.

Jerry steers us back on our course south-southwest. *Mud and Blood* fills with a crackle and whip. Impelled by the wind, *Hoop* picks up speed, heels and settles into a broad reach. Roused by the commotion, Johanna appears.

'Papa, turn the engines off,' she says, all tousle-haired and haughty. 'I can't think.'

'Whatever you say, my little countess,' Arno replies, 'although back in the old country, thinking is not to be encouraged in a lady.'

'Papa, you are such an old dinosaur. With our fortune and lands all stolen, what can a girl do except get an education?' Before her father can reply, she adds, 'And don't say find a husband!'

Bending to Johanna's will to make his life easier, Arno stops the engines. From the noise of pumping pistons to the gentle ripple of sails, there is a moment of transformation as diesel fumes evaporate and the elements take over. Using only nature's wind and a large spread of canvas, *Hoop* shows a lively turn of speed.

'Now she's talking,' I mutter, relishing the sensation as waves glance off the hull with a sound like chattering children. Looking along the deck, Lucie's working hard sheeting in the mainsail with a powerful winch. She moves quickly between tasks until the well-trimmed sails transform *Hoop* from a motorsailer into a racing yacht. Lucie takes over Jerry's helm with independence and self-belief. She's authentic, windblown—a poster girl for a 1970s feminist manifesto.

Soon, she calls me up to show me how *Hoop* performs under sail. Under a protective windscreen are the gimbal compass, depth and speed indicators, and the engine controls. A fold-down seat allows whoever is on the helm to sit or stand. With good all-around visibility, *Hoop*'s cockpit is higher than the deck, and few areas of a ship have more uses than the cockpit of an offshore sailboat, be it lounging about on a quiet day at anchor or managing a fast-moving situation at sea. After an hour's excitement and exhilaration at handling her, I go below, leaving fifty imperial tons of sailboat in Lucie's capable hands. If Freddy Fate is playing cards today, he's dealing me aces.

***

Descending the broad teak ladder from the cockpit feels like stepping into another realm. The sounds of the ocean and the wind fade, replaced by the creak of the boat. Through the portholes, sparkles of sunlight cast patterns over a spacious saloon. *Hoop* isn't merely a boat; she's a sanctuary, a floating home for the family during their global wanderings.

At its heart is a large table surrounded by banquette seats. With a savoury aroma wafting from the galley, it's easy to imagine the laughter and ruckus that have bubbled up as Anna conjures meals for her hungry brood. Located near the companionway, the Captain's navigation station, scattered with various charts and instruments, resembles a puzzle that begs to be solved. Tucked away in a quiet nook, a quarter berth is my bunk.

Anna reassures me when I prod the foam mattress, 'You will be comfortable here. It's snug. I sleep here myself if Arno is snoring.'

'Don't worry,' I assure her. 'I've been travelling for the past year. I can sleep just about anywhere.'

'I'm so glad you could come,' she says, securing the porthole. 'When we were in Europe, this boat seemed safe, but out here, once the other crew left…' She pauses, there is a moment of vulnerability.

I blunder into the gap. 'It's not every day you have so many women on a boat.'

'We had a boy, but he died young.' She straightens my berth with motherly kindness. 'He would have been your age. Arno misses not having a son around.'

Anna's talk is down-to-earth, openly addressing a painful issue rather than beating around the bush. It's awkward being confronted with such honesty.

'Isn't it funny how I've ended up here after you asked me to join you in Antigua, and I couldn't decide whether to come along or not?'

'Yes!' She brightens. 'It's as though it's meant to be.'

'Did you ever see *Gay Gander* again?' I ask, knowing Arno and Anna hit it off with my earlier skipper and his partner on the two occasions we'd met up coming across the Atlantic.

'John and Carola returned a few days after we saw you in Antigua on New Year's Eve, but you had disappeared.'

'If I'd stayed, I would have drunk myself stupid,' I say, remembering how sorry for myself I was at being unceremoniously dismissed. 'Did they ask after me?'

'They wanted to check you were all right. They enjoy their new life together and recognize they would never have made it without your help. I think they felt guilty at abandoning you.'

'They kicked me off the boat two days after we crossed the Atlantic,' I say, surprising myself with how emotionally charged the memory is. I change the subject. 'Is that when you met Jerry?'

Anna nods. 'With pirates hijacking yachts to run drugs, we decided an ex-serviceman on board would be wise. Arno grew up in Austria during the war, so he and Jerry talk the same language.'

My eyes widen in disbelief—maybe there is a Nazi connection. 'With the children our precious cargo, we must return unscathed.'

'You must be looking forward to going home. After all, there's nothing like the comfort of familiar surroundings, especially after a journey like yours.'

Anna is wistful. 'For me, home is three places. Holland, the war-ruined homeland I fled at age eighteen, Canada, where I raised my Kinder and this boat. I am always at home but never ever there.'

'All sounds rather complicated.'

'Life goes that way after a while,' she ruffles her straight, home-cut hair to rub the idea out of her head. 'Where is your home?'

'England,' I say, generalizing.

'No! Your home?' She wants to find out where I come from.

'Nowhere anymore,' I say, realizing my words sound ridiculous. I try to put them into context as much for myself as for Anna. 'I'm footloose, fancy-free and curious to discover the world inch by inch.'

'What about your parents? Do they know where you are?'

This obvious question is one I'm embarrassed to answer. 'Divorced,' I blurt it out as though it's an ugly word. 'They both have new lives where I don't fit in, and new houses where I don't belong.'

'What a terrible thing!' Anna says. 'It could never happen to Arno and me. We are inseparable.' She repeats the word 'divorce' as if trying to understand it. 'Well, this is your home right now,' she pats the bed as she knows it's a respite from insecurity. 'Since we can't get to where we'd rather be, we must make the best of where we are.'

I stow my gear after Anna leaves me in the no-man's land of the quarter berth. Apart from deck wear, including my smelly but much-loved alpaca sweater, I own a linen suit, silk shirt, *I Ching*, passport, logbook, and money. My cramped quarters are by the hatch but out of the way. Getting in and out will require gymnastics if needed on deck in a hurry. Due to its position, I imagine it is the wettest place on the yacht in heavy weather but the safest place in a rolling sea. Modest though my newfound berth is, it's a home. Wriggling in it is surprisingly comfortable—how fortunes change. Last night, I was alone like the *Lone Ranger*. Now, I'm with a modern-day version of the *Swiss Family Robinson*.

***

'Ten minutes until your watch,' Lucie says, prodding me awake, torch in hand. Squinting in the beam of light, I struggle to remember where I am. 'What time is it?'

'Four in the morning. You've been asleep for ages.'

'Was I snoring?' I ask, gradually getting my bearings.

'No, snuffling a little.' Pushing the torchlight away, I inquire about the difference. 'One's annoying, the other's endearing,' she says, disappearing up the companionway.

Extracting myself from my new lodgings takes me a moment, but it may be easier with practice. I once slept on the luggage rack of a train—it's no different trying to roll out of this berth.

Pulling on my faithful sweater and stepping into the cockpit, I notice Lucie's face lit by the dim compass light. Above us is a crescent moon and an abundance of stars. With the sound of wind in the sails, I'm back in the enchanted world of Planet Ocean.

'Neptune's in a good mood tonight,' I say, scanning the horizon for the light of other vessels.

'And we're all alone,' my companion answers, one hand resting lazily on the wheel. 'I love sailing at night when luminous shimmering trails dance playfully beside us and leave a glimmering path in our wake.' Enthralled, I listen to Lucie rhapsodizing, her voice as seductive as the silver sickle moon casting its cool light across the nape of her neck.

Lucie has *Hoop* running at night speed—nothing pressured, just safe and steady. She is an accomplished sailor with thousands of sea miles behind her, so I'm nervous when it's my turn to steer because I'm only used to a tiller.

Hoop's wheel has eight spokes with an added notch on the king shaft, allowing you to gauge the rudder angle in the dark. I start to oversteer with knee-jerk reactions as the vagaries of the swell take me by surprise. The mark of good helming is a clean wake—mine resembles a drunken sailor's rolling gait.

'You'll have us all seasick that way,' Lucie says. 'We're reaching, so be gentle on the wheel. You're guiding, not steering.' Her voice is a mix of caution and allure. She tilts her head and smiles. 'You know how to be gentle, don't you?' It's like the Bacall and Bogart moment in *To Have and Have Not*, where Slim shows Steve how to whistle. 'Let the wind do all the hard work, or you won't last the week.'

We sail on in silence until the sky gradually lightens behind us, and the horizon sharpens in the baby blue of morning. It takes the crack of dawn to make me wake up to the fact, that, no matter how much I want this watch to go on forever, you can't hold back time.

When Lucie leaves me alone on the helm to go and wake Johanna and Jerry for their stint, I feel she trusts me. Lost in reverie, I trace the wheel spokes and feel a growing sense of direction, as though I've found my moral compass.

***

After catching some Z's, I'm back on deck as Arno calls a confab.

'Now listen up, crew,' He clears his throat. 'We've made over three hundred nautical miles. Our course for the next week will be a bearing of two hundred and forty-five degrees from here to Panama.' Then, after a brief pause for dramatic effect. 'Where's the danger in that?'

Hoping to prove my worth, my hand shoots up like an eager schoolboy. 'Monotony leads to complacency.' I parrot a former skipper who had drummed this into me.

'Precisely! We can't afford any accidents, so stay alert, or we'll end up in a pickle.'

'What! worse than Mama's sauerkraut?' Johanna chips in, bringing a bit of humor to the situation.

'Mick, you'll oversee all the running gear before the mainmast. First mate, your responsibility is aft. Mickie, your job as a rigging monkey is double-checking the standing rigging and…'

'No need to tell me mine,' Lucie interrupts.

Arno pushes back his straight dark hair, that occasionally falls over a brainy-looking forehead. 'I hate to admit it, Lucie, but no one can sail *Hoop* better than you.' He scrutinizes Jerry and me. 'Expect a hard mistress.'

Jerry elbows me in the ribs. 'I can live with that,' he whispers. 'And what's her job?' He nods towards Johanna.

'She gets to tell you when you're not doing yours,' Arno replies as though it's an old joke.

'With you all busy with your chores, someone must play passenger. Otherwise, what's the point of going anywhere?

'Like the army,' Jerry says. 'You'll always find a shirker.'

'Not so fast, soldier.' Johanna gives him a wink. 'I'm available to rub sun lotion on the parts you can't reach.'

'Oh, my gawd,' groans Lucie. 'Pass the sick bag.'

'Enough, already,' Anna chides from the hatch. 'It's lunchtime.' She passes up a tray of sausage and sauerkraut sandwiches and our last ration of fresh milk.

With the cockpit transformed into a makeshift diner, we bask in the warmth of each other's company. Our sense of camaraderie is palpable as we finish eating and seamlessly fall back into our roles. The cloudless sky above reflects the mood on board: we are now a proper crew.

With such a steady wind, Anna warns us of the perils of windburn, so lashings of sun lotion are squeezed around, and Jerry has his back anointed by Johanna. When it comes to my turn and the near-empty bottle makes a flatulent noise, Mickie accuses me of farting and holds her nose. I sense jolly japes ahead.

***

With the privilege of the off-duty man and institutionally idle until given an order, Jerry spends the afternoon fishing from the back of the boat. He has a sports rod strapped to the taffrail and is trolling a lure a hundred feet behind us. Even though the bait tumbles rather than skips along the surface, Jerry remains optimistic. He believes we're going too fast to catch anything, but adopts a 'nothing ventured, nothing gained' attitude. In moments of downtime, Jerry finds it best to try his luck, even if the odds are against him. Anna is keen to have fresh fish as a healthy addition to the vegetables and dumplings planned for supper. She also needs the girls to find out where food comes from and not be squeamish about preparing it. Due to poor eyesight and having lost her glasses along the way, Anna doesn't take a watch, but she's as happy in the galley as a Dutch woman in a Vermeer painting.

The day drags on until a commotion erupts at the back of the boat when the fishing reel screams out on its ratchet like a swarm of angry bees. Jerry, who's been dozing against the mizzen mast, is up and at it like a shot. Johanna shouts for everyone to come and look. Mickie pushes past, scrambling for a closer inspection; she leaps onto the taffrail and yells for Arno's binoculars.

The anticipation grows as Jerry plays the rod, managing the reel tension like a pro. He can't even believe his eyes when he sees what's on the hook. With a clear view of the quarry, Arno laughs first. 'We have no fish for our dish but a fouled fowl,' he says, the glasses pointing up rather than down as the line is no longer in the water but attached to a living kite.

'Bugger,' curses Jerry, trying to reel in the reluctant bird. While he knows how to cope with the run and dive of a fish, trying to play a pelican with a six-foot wingspan swirling thirty feet overhead is a different skill.

The keen-eyed predator must have seen the bait and plunge-dived from over sixty feet to catch what it had hoped was a fish. Only after surfacing and draining water from its gullet did it take to the air, snared to the boat. The fishing line is too strong to break and too precious to waste by cutting—which would only condemn the bird to death—so Jerry slowly brings it down while Anna grabs her camera, eager to capture the absurdity of the moment.

The poor creature appears furious when Jerry hauls it alongside, and I hang over the boarding gate to land the beast. Surprisingly light for its size, it doesn't fight until I land it on the deck, when it pecks me as I grasp its snout and get a cut from the sharp edges of its hooked beak. Mickie's instinct is to put her sun hat over the bird's eyes to disorientate it. Once subdued, Jerry cuts off the barb by pushing the hook through the pouch and snipping it off.

'Mama, can I keep it as a pet?' Mickie asks, wanting to cuddle her absurd-looking hat stand.

'No, Vögelchen,' Anna's affection shines through. 'It must be set free. Free as you are, free as a bird.'

After examining its wings for injury, I let the creature back onto the water, where it bobs about, looking bemused by the incident. Mickie waves goodbye while I recite a ditty learned as a boy.

A wonderful bird is the pelican.
His beak can hold more than his belly can.
He can hold in his beak enough food for a week.
But I'll be damned if I can see how the helican.

***

We all fall into the rhythm of a long passage and bond together as crewmates. Day and night meld seamlessly, the relentless breeze blowing hairdryer hot. Even the cotton candy clouds hang in the sky, reluctant to change.

In this liquid continuum of sea and sky, where time stretches and bends, our concerns narrow down to the spartan life of eating, sleeping, and keeping watch. It's a peculiar and enchanting existence where the yacht's gentle motion and the unending horizon are the only constants in our surreal reality.

By the sixth day, we've reached the 14th parallel, acclimatizing to the weather and each other's quirks. Jerry's penchant for long toenails, my unconscious humming of a tune off-key, and the girls' inclination for nudity become ticks and irritations.

In spite of Anna's attempts to engage us with maintenance tasks—rubbing down, varnishing the brightwork, and making repairs—the oppressive heat wraps around us like a stifling blanket, inducing a languor typical of extended voyages. Aside from keeping an eye on the empty sea for some sign of life, my only amusement is seeing Lucie navigate using sails alone, skillfully avoiding the need to steer.

Nonetheless, the spell breaks when she finishes her watch, as without her subtle control, *Hoop* starts to bridle. I untie the helm, trying to match her efficiency. We slip into the night. The wind drops. Lucie will have made the most progress in today's odyssey.

***

'Mick!' Anna calls out from the galley. 'Come here.'

Quick as a flash, both Mickie and I are standing next to her.

'Which one?' I ask, bemused, as both of us have appeared.

Mickie jumps up and down. 'Bet it was me!'

'This is ridiculous,' Anna laughs, arms akimbo. 'I only want one.'

Arno is also amused. 'What's the saying? You wait ages for a bus, and two turn up.' He then starts explaining random matrix theory.

While I'm attentive to Professor Arno outlining probability

distribution, Mickie is beside herself with impatience. 'Papa, stop it! Mama, which one of us do you want for what?'

Now totally bewildered, Anna stares at us both. 'I can't remember. I really can't remember.'

'The solution to the problem so this doesn't happen again,' Arno says, looking at me. 'Is to give this Mick a nickname.'

Anna likes the suggestion. 'Good idea! Go and ask Lucie. She has a pet name for everyone.'

'What's mine?' Arno asks. Anna turns to him as Mickie leads me away. 'You don't want to know.'

Heading aft, I'm reticent about the idea. My nicknames in the past haven't been complimentary, one being 'Boom Boom!' on account of my loud voice, and another bestowed at school, 'Thick Mick,' because teachers thought me stupid.

In the girls' cabin, it's stiflingly hot, and as I peer through the door, they are lying spreadeagled, wearing next to nothing. Johanna makes no effort to cover herself up. 'Crew are not allowed in here,' she says in a haughty tone.

Ignoring her, Mickie drags me in. 'Lucie! Mama's all confused with two Micks on board. We've got to find this Mick a nickname.'

'Jackass,' suggests Johanna.

'Thanks a lot!' I say, giving her the bird. 'Don't I have a say?'

'Don't be stupid,' she says, rolling onto her front and wiggling her feet in the air, the curve of her bottom as perfect as a pair of burger buns. 'No one ever chooses their nickname.'

'What's it to be?' Mickie's impatient. 'Mama's waiting.'

'According to Jerry, he's a fruit,' Johanna says.

'What do you mean?' I say, shocked to find he's spreading rumors behind my back.

'You've got a camp voice. All fruity and sort of plummy.'

After deep thought, Lucie sits up with her arms wrapped around her knees. Her facial expression changes as if she has solved a crossword puzzle. 'Let's call him Plum.'

'Or bum,' Mickie snickers.

'Plum it is then!' I say, overheating from the proximity of the girls' warm-scented bodies.

'Plum Bum! Plum Bum! Plum Bum!' Mickie repeats over and over till I grab her and try to tickle her into silence. Lucie clobbers me with a cushion, and the cabin erupts into a pillow fight. When I pin Lucie down, our eyes meet blue on blue. Hers are oceans deep, and as I fall into their mysterious depths, I'm taken aback by an eerie feeling, as though we met in an earlier incarnation. Then Mickie jumps on my back, and Lucie squirms out of my grasp.

'Children, what a noise!' Anna scolds, peering through the cabin door, ending the fun. 'And what a mess you've made.'

'It's nothing to do with me,' Johanna says, distancing herself from such childish activities. 'And when are we going to be in Panama? This trip is so boring,' she adds, as though out of spite.

'Mickey's now called Plum,' Lucie confirms.

'Plum Bum. Plum Bum,' Mickie insists.

'That will do,' Anna chides. 'Papa's spotted dolphins.'

All the girls scamper out of the cabin like puppies, and I straighten things up. Jerry appears.

'Plumping up the cushions. Bit of a giveaway, mate.'

***

By late afternoon, bare, barrel-chested Arno is at the helm, happily humming to himself. His daughters play cards on the cabin roof while Anna rustles up supper below. On the aft deck, Jerry and I fall into the camaraderie of the bunker. We discuss sleeping arrangements as he's berthed in the single cabin beside the girls.

'They talk between themselves in German. I'm certain it's about me.' Leaning back against the mizzen mast, he has an air of conceit about him. I want to burst his bubble.

'Probably not. I doubt you're even on their radar.'

'Come on, you might not fancy them, but they're the classiest birds you'll ever meet. No wonder the other guys didn't last. I bet they reported them for wanking too loud.'

'Hey, let's remember we're both here to do a job, but if you want to be Casanova—carry on.'

'That's the difference between us,' Jerry sniffs. 'You're a soft poof, but fuckin' and fightin' are my middle names.'

It's my chance to find out more about Jerry. 'What did you do in the army? In Antigua, you told me you were in the SAS.'

Giving himself time to think, he slips the commando knife from the sheath on his belt. 'No one in the special forces will ever tell you

24

they are or the first thing about it. The only time you'll ever find out is when you're knocking on the Pearly Gates.' Picking up a whetstone, he spits onto it, 'I say it to impress people.'

'Did you ever serve in the forces then, or is it bullshit?'

He pauses and slowly sharpens the blade. 'I was an armorer in the infantry in Northern Ireland. Made it to lance-jack,' His jaw follows the slow rotation of his hands as he works up the edges of the cold steel. 'I was deployed in Belfast where nobody had any fucking idea of what we should be doing.'

'What is the IRA like?' I knew 'The Troubles' had seen hundreds of dead from bombs, bullets, and extra-judicial killings. 'They seem so callous.'

'Cold-hearted killers, men who are part idealists, part gangsters. Our mission was to prevent the Orangies and Shinners from tearing each other apart, but we ended up caught in the middle.'

'Must have been exciting, though.' My comment's crass, but sometimes I wish I'd gone into the army.

Jerry scoffs. 'We had to round up anyone suspected of being a Republican. It meant going into houses at dawn, dragging men from their beds while their wives and children stood in the doorway spitting and screaming at you.' A vein on his forehead pulses as he speaks. 'Not exactly what I'd signed up for.' He assesses the keenness of the blade. 'If living on your nerves and seeing everything as a booby trap is what you call exciting, then it was.'

I gaze out to sea, absorbing Jerry's account of his nerve-wracking experiences and living with hidden dangers.

Out of the blue, Jerry redirects the conversation. 'What are you going to do when we get to Canada?'

Caught off guard, I respond, 'No idea.'

A sly grin plays on Jerry's face as he probes further, 'So you came along for the free ride.'

'Sort of.'

His next question puts me on the spot, 'How are you going to make money?'

I offer a vague reply, 'I've got a bit to tide me over.'

But Jerry, ever the wheeler and dealer, sees an opportunity. 'Want to invest?'

I'm perplexed. 'What in?'

His response is enigmatic, 'Don't know yet. But keep your money close at hand. There'll be an opportunity somewhere along the way.'

***

Climbing down the companionway stairs after our heads up, I bang my head against the hatch.

'Been there since the boat was built and always will be,' Mickie chuckles. 'One day, you'll learn to duck, knucklehead.'

With no younger sibling of my own, having Mickie around is fun. Even if, as in this case, she's a precocious and irritating little brat with no intention of doing what others expect of her. Possibly, this is why '*Mein kleiner Wildfang*', appears to be Arno's favourite.

'Do you want to witness some magic?' she says, wriggling on the saloon banquette to get comfortable.

Humoring her, I sit down. 'I'm always up for a trick.'

'It's not a trick. It's magic!' She corrects me, shuffling a pack with all the skill of a card sharp and fanning the blue-and-white-backed deck out in front of me. 'Pick a card, any card!'

From then on, I'm in thrall to a consummate professional as her nimble fingers precisely move the cards.

'How did you do that?' I implore as she spreads the deck before me and points to my chosen card.

'A magician never reveals her secrets,' she says, cocksure and enjoying my amazement. 'Besides, it's magic.'

'Yea! Yea!' I reply as she mixes the playing cards and goes into another pick-a-card trick.

Unseen by her, my card is the Seven of Diamonds. She shuffles the pack and tells me to stretch out my hand.

'Hold the pack between your thumb and forefinger,' she says, adjusting my grip. 'Not too loose, not too tight.'

In the same way as a dutiful stooge, I do as I'm told.

'Abracadabra!' Mickie slaps her hand down smartly on the back of the pack. All cards, bar one, fall onto the table. I turn it over. Dumbfounded, I gawk at seven diamond shapes staring back at me.

She triumphantly pushes the cards onto the floor, chirruping, 'So long, sucker! Clear them up,' before scampering out on deck.

Scrambling under the table, I'm astonished at how a child hijacked my mind and made me believe things that are illusions. Learning how gullible people are so young, I wonder what her future will be.

'You've got a real firecracker there,' I say as Anna hands me an elastic band from a jar, saved by someone who knows shortages. Similar to the mother in *Swiss Family Robinson*, Anna's foresight in saving things shows she's frugal and resourceful in a family with as many members.

'The future needs feisty women, and my job is to supply three of them,' she says proudly.

With a dynastic legacy at stake, in a world where a tomboy is no legal substitute for a male heir, I can only guess at the marital strain with no chance of more children.

'Is that why you took Mickie out of school to teach them yourself?'

'Yes! Travel lets you grow culturally, makes you a more interesting person, and helps you develop virtues like patience and humility.' Anna sits down as she wants to talk. 'Canada is a young country and egalitarian, but I married a count, and my girls are blue-blood stock from Austro-Hungarian aristocracy.'

'But didn't that all finish after the First World War?' I ask, surprised Anna sounds like snob as the words countess and humility are unusual bedfellows.

'This century has been a disaster for Arno's family. The Socialists broke up the empire. Nationalists seized the family property, and the Communists stole the rest. All my girls have left is the title. Beauty is a temporary visa to a bright future. A good name is a passport.'

'It must be difficult, though, with all the other things going on,' I say, ever more amazed by the people I'm travelling with.

'The endless juggle of fitting in lessons is the hardest part of the trip. Sailing increases self-awareness and confidence, but the lessons boost creativity and imagination.'

'And they are all bilingual?'

'Trilingual!' she says, almost affronted.

'Mickie said she speaks four!'

'Let's call the last one an exaggeration!'

A freshening breeze starts blowing through the saloon, with cooler air picked up from somewhere far away. We sit, enjoying the fleeting relief from the heat. I break our silence after *Hoop* rides a wave and the cups in the galley rattle.

'How did you find your way to Canada?'

'I emigrated from a war-torn homeland.'

'What was it like in Holland during the occupation?'

'The invasion brought jobs, but as the war progressed, Germany demanded more for less until nothing was left.

'What happened after the D-Day landings?' I persist, ignorant of the Low Countries apart from what I've seen in war films.

'The Germans held out until the end of the war. Nearly eight thousand Canadians died trying to liberate us.'

'Is that why you went to Canada afterward?' I ask. Anna explains how the Dutch and Canadian governments signed an agreement to bring families over, increasing the country's rural population.

'How did you cope with moving so far and starting with nothing?'

'Being scared of arrest for no reason takes your breath away. Once you can breathe again, any hardship is bearable.'

'And you were sent to British Columbia?'

'They welcomed me, but it's a cultural wilderness. People only talk about the mountains. It's not enough for my girls. They must not be dull housewives to dull husbands.'

'From what I can tell, they've a head start,' I say. 'All have wings.'

'Forget any foolishness about them being pushy. I want my girls to be free and heard. Closed mouths don't get fed.'

'You want them to be free!'

'Yes! The same as here at sea, living without fear or compulsion. You can't put a price on freedom.'

Anna returns to the galley to make supper. She is not only a loving mother who keeps her family afloat but a woman full of humanity and strength of character—I'm already putting her on a pedestal.

***

After supper, Johanna cries off sick, claiming Code Red, so I stand in for her night watch with Arno. We're getting close to land, and the skipper's a little on edge as the quarter moon sets at midnight and a sea mist has risen, limiting our visibility. He's relying on the radar—a new navigation tool to learn. He shows me how to remove clutter so the cursor sweeping around the fluorescent green display highlights solid objects, not extraneous stuff like rain or waves.

'These two targets here.' Arno points to two dots pulsing like heartbeats. 'Ships travelling in a convoy, and we will pass between them as I don't want to change course.'

'Our eyes in the dark,' I say in the gloom. Missing only the ping of sonar, the war movie *The Cruel Sea* comes to mind.

'Without the radar, we would have never seen them in this mist,' he says, working out the bearing line.

'The British invented radar during the war,' I say proudly.

'Yes! But we made it better through German efficiency.'

Arno's use of 'we' raises my hackles. Every British schoolboy knows, *we* won the war. We won it through pluck and determination in spite of the odds. We won it against *them*. I've never met one of *them* before, and here is one of *them* calling himself *we*—and I like him. One after another, my certainties are turned upside down.

'Didn't help you in the end,' I reply petulantly.

'Young man!' Arno turns, his glasses reflecting the pulsating blips on the radar screen—inching closer. 'What you were taught is a comic book version of events.' His tone is serious. 'I was ten when Hitler marched into Austria and eighteen when the Russians invaded.'

Listening to Arno speak, I realize I'm hearing the other side of the story, a firsthand account from a man with skin in the game.

'After the Third Reich annexed the Sudetenland, my father, heir to titles and lands, supported the regime.' Arno's voice is tinged with grief. 'But war changes everything. It shatters illusions, upends traditions, and turns the world upside down.'

'What about the land?'

'At the end of the war the Soviets seized everything. But I am about to restore our fortune and family name; it needed someone to die first.' He stops abruptly as our midnight talk crosses a line.

'Go forward and see what you can see,' he says, handing me the binoculars, concerned at the behaviour of the targets on the radar.

At the prow, I peer through the glasses, trying to penetrate the moving wraiths of mist. Through the haze, I spot a long, low object ahead. Then it strikes me. It's a supertanker returning two signals, one from its bow and one from the stern. We are heading amidships.

'Hard to starboard! We're on a collision course.'

Arno bears away. I run back to ease the mainsheet to stop the sail from backing, then quickly let out the headsail. Disaster averted, the quarter-mile-long vessel slides by and *Hoop* dances in her wake.

Arno plays down the closeness of our shave. 'I doubt there's anyone on the bridge— probably all asleep.'

Oblivious to us, the tanker forges on. The stern light shrinks to a pinprick, disappearing but for the smell of lube oil lingering in the air. The rule of the sea is that power gives way to sail, but a tanker takes a mile to change course. With no umpire to call foul, our wreckage wouldn't be noticed. I try not to dwell on what could have happened.

'Let's keep this to ourselves.' Arno's chest is rising and falling in short breaths. 'Our little secret. No need to worry the women.'

Chapter 2

Panama Red

After ten days at sea, driven by the persistent push of the trade winds, the silhouette of the Canal Zone's breakwater appears on the horizon. A collective cheer erupts as we slip behind its protective barrier, and *Hoop*'s roll, pitch, and yaw subside.

Arno's voice crackles over the VHF radio, announcing our impending arrival. Amid this orchestrated activity, we spring into action, stowing sails and tidying lines with practiced efficiency. Amidst the hustle and bustle, I have a special duty: raising the Stars and Stripes and the Panamanian courtesy flags. This seemingly simple act symbolizes our formal entry into the Canal Zone, where American ownership and Panamanian interests entwine. When I hoist the flags, a profound sense of pride wells up within me, a tribute to what I've achieved to get here. I feel a little taller.

Arno summons us all to the cockpit. 'We must wait a few days for our transit date to be assigned.'

'Which means a chance to go ashore and let off steam,' Anna adds, looking forward to respite from us all.

'Somewhere, a cold beer has my name on it,' Jerry chips in. I share the sentiment. Johanna craves iced tea. For Lucie and Mickie, snow cones are the answer. Together we stand on the deck, parched with thirst, dreaming of treats on dry land tomorrow.

***

Motoring towards Colón, Panama's Atlantic-facing city, the cargo ships waiting in line to transit the Canal dwarf *Hoop* and the visual impact of a structure that I only imagined from a long-ago geography lesson sinks in. Ahead of us lies a vast maritime complex overshadowing anything I have ever seen. Escaping the busy shipping channel, Arno negotiates the shifting sandbar mentioned in the pilot manual, and we head for the Panama Canal Yacht Club to tie up close to its plantation-style clubhouse.

After Arno exchanges formalities with the authorities, the girls, accustomed to a week of bucket and flannel baths on the aft deck, are quickly off to find the hot showers. Still on our wobbly sea legs, Jerry and I set off to explore the Canal Zone, glad to be away from them. From the yacht club's marina, we walk through well-ordered streets resembling a home away from home. Despite two red-and-white-chequered water towers dominating the skyline like creatures from *The War of the Worlds*, the place resembles any midwestern American town. The Canal Zone is an unincorporated territory, so it's administered by but not part of the United States.

'If I had a camera, I could make you look like a giant,' I say to Jerry as we stop by a miniature Statue of Liberty.

'And if that was open, I could make you look like a loser,' he challenges me, pointing to a bowling alley. 'This is all amazing.

Compared with our military bases, these guys are pampered harem eunuchs. The British Army is all about spartan conditions and harsh discipline. I don't reckon you could fight after this soft treatment.'

After writing and posting an airmail to my sister at the post office, we then join the girls for lunch in the clubhouse. We enjoy juicy burgers and hot fries, washing them down with ice-cold root beer. Mickie devours an ice cream soda with a spoon as long as her arm.

Afterward, Jerry challenges me to a game of golf on the nine-hole course visitors can use. Johanna tags along, though we're unsure of the rules or even which one of the borrowed clubs to use first. Born with poor hand-eye coordination, I've never enjoyed the pantheon of pleasures ballgames offer. The rub of this green feels all too familiar.

'You're supposed to address the ball, not stare it to death,' Johanna says, impatient at my delay.

For the second time, I swing and miss. 'This is harder than it looks,' I cry in frustration, making another attempt. Amazingly, this time my club connects, and the ball lands twenty feet away, followed by a sod of turf dug up as a divot.

'Well, it's a start,' Jerry says, pushing me aside.

'Just not a promising one,' Johanna adds, eager to take another shot at her ball, which landed way up the fairway.

Jerry curses as he slices his drive. We wander around, swishing at balls, getting nowhere. After a while, Johanna becomes bored, hijacks the golf buggy, and careens off.

'Come back,' Jerry shouts. 'The club only allows men to drive!'

'Sexist remarks won't help your handicap. I'm already up to par,' she yells back, narrowly avoiding a bunker.

Waving a seven-iron at her, Jerry searches for his ball while I wait on the fairway, listening to bird calls and trying to catch a glimpse of flitting feathers in the foliage.

'Can't find it,' he grumbles. 'This game's for the birds.'

'That one probably stole it.' I point out a toucan hopping from branch to branch. It's a comical sight with an enormous, coloured beak and a call that sounds as though it's trying to scold the world.

Hauling our gear back to the clubhouse, we meet a sizable iguana feasting on a ripe mango that has fallen from a burgeoning tree. It regards us with reptilian smugness, aware that it is safe from being slaughtered by the locals and served with a plate of black beans and rice, as Yanks aren't the type to exchange their burgers for *tree chicken*. Foraging, I pluck six pendulous fruits to stash in the golf bag to take back to the boat.

On our way, I spot Johanna and Lucie sitting on a bleacher by the baseball ground. Nearby, Mickie is hanging off a pole like a baboon, her eyes wide with pleasure and her face a broad grin.

'Where's the buggy?' Fearing the worst.

'Some officious little dick took it off me,' Johanna replies, full of insouciant indignation. 'He said something about not driving it across the green.' She gestures towards the course with extended arms. 'It's all green here. How am I supposed to tell the difference?'

'Come on, you guys!' urges Mickie, dropping to the ground. 'Let's play hide-and-seek.'

'Sod that!' says Jerry. 'I'm going for a beer.'

'Plum, you be the seeker,' says Lucie, rising to the thrill of the chase. 'And no sneak peeks.' Hand in hand, she and Mickie runoff.

Reluctant to appear too eager, Johanna comes over and whispers, 'Shut those big blue eyes, count to ten, and find me first.'

As instructed, I count the numbers out loud, then blink back into the sunlight to find that the girls have vanished. 'Ready or not, here I come.' In the gymnasium building opposite, a door slams.

Creeping inside an area signposted as the Tumbling and Wrestling Room, that smells of polished linoleum, I spot Johanna poorly concealed behind a door. 'Gotcha!' I exclaim.

She pushes the door closed.

'So now you've found me. What will you do?' My senses go into overload. Is this a test, a tease, a come-on?

'Find the others!' I say, trying not to be drawn in.

'Jerry says you're not attracted to women,' she whispers, getting closer. 'I'm not sure I believe him.'

'Who knows?' I reply, but then the devil gets my tongue, and I add, 'You're still a girl.'

Quick as a flash, her hand lashes out, catching me with a stinging blow across the left cheek. 'Remember who you're talking to,' she hisses. 'I'm a countess, and don't you forget it.' Then, pushing me away, she walks outside and shouts to the others, 'Mickie! Lucie! The game's over. We'd best be getting back. Plum couldn't find the fairy on a Christmas tree!'

Smarting, I head off to the clubhouse bar. Seeing my red cheek, Jerry splutters into his beer.

'Cor blimey, mate, who hit you?'

'Johanna! The cat has claws.'

'Mischievous little minx!' He examines my face. 'No harm done. Get this beer down you and come and meet Scott. He's a true-born Zonian and will take us to a party tonight at the Tarpon Club. Also,' Jerry adds, tapping his nose in the universal code for confidentiality. 'While we're here, we might do some business together.'

***

When we return to the boat several beers later, I discover Arno and Anna have deaf ears to melodrama as they ignore the girls' fury when they find out Jerry and I are off to have fun without them.

'It's only for serious golfers,' Jerry teases Johanna.

'It's a men-only club,' I add, my tone fawning.

'That would suit you,' she sneers, bridling at the macho posturing.

I rub my slapped cheek. The failure to come-on to her has confirmed Jerry's slander, so in her eyes, I'm queer. It may prove a convenient smokescreen with two headstrong girls on board. With Johanna looking daggers and threatening revenge, Jerry and I escape and head off, the very picture of sailors on shore leave.

'Where's this party, then?'

'There isn't one. It was an excuse to get us ashore.'

'Well, what are we going to do.'

Jerry stops and eyeballs me. It's a stare I can't avoid. 'You didn't have the guts to be a drug runner in Antigua. But here, if we pool our resources, which I hope you've got with you, we'll make serious cash.'

'How?' I ask, intrigued though knowing I should say 'No!' to whatever he suggests.

Jerry snaps his fingers with hypnotic precision. 'It's a simple equation. Marijuana grows here. Where we're going, it doesn't.'

'What's your plan?' I hear myself saying.

'The guy I met earlier can sell us some Panama Red.'

'Holy shit!' When Jerry suggested running drugs, I didn't think he'd already met someone with the best weed in the world.'

'It's dirt cheap here.'

Knowing Jerry of old, I'm wary and sense a trap; I fix him eye-to-eye. 'Why do you need me?'

The question catches Jerry off guard, and his eyes dart away momentarily before meeting my gaze again. He takes a deep breath and carries on in a more persuasive tone.

'Now, I can tell you're wary. But trust me, this is a great opportunity for both of us. I need your money to buy a decent amount of product, and then I'll need your help getting it onto the boat. We can work together to find a buyer in Canada. We'll split the profits, and you'll come out ahead. We need each other for this to work.' He extends his hand to seal the deal. 'Are you up for a caper this time, partner?'

'It's risky. Who is this guy. What if he's setting us up?'

Jerry laughs. 'Don't be stupid; he's a Yank who wants to make a quick buck.' His hand hovers in front of me, beckoning.

'Yes, but what about getting it into Canada on the other end?

'We've got the perfect cover,' he exclaims. 'The family will be greeted as returning heroes. Nobody's liable to suspect them of something illegal. Think about it, mate. There'll never be another chance as easy as this.'

'I not sure, Jerry. We're putting them in danger.'

'Well, I'm no stranger to danger.' He pins me with his eyes. 'Be realistic, they're not paying you. You'll be dumped at the end of the voyage. How much of your arse have you got left to peddle?'

A moral dilemma unfolds before me—conflicting feelings of alienating Jerry or doing right by the family.

Jerry's argument about money gains the upper hand. He's right; after this voyage, I'll have nothing but the shirt on my back. My usual wishful thinking while avoiding the consequences pushes me to a reckless decision.

'I'm in!'

We seal our deal with a handshake. It's not just a partnership; it's a stake in a future fraught with risk.

Emboldened by my answer, Jerry sets off at the double. I struggle to keep up as the idea of becoming an international drug smuggler takes hold. In no time, we come to a boulevard where the palm trees have white-painted bases, and everything is spick-and-span.

'You found it all right?' Scott says, coming down the red-brick steps of the Young Men's Christian Association.

'Not hard,' Jerry replies. 'It's the biggest building for miles.'

'Let me give you the tour.' Scott walks us to his red VW Beetle.

Before long, we're driving down a coast road in the slug-bug to the crackle of the American Forces Radio blaring out 'Chimes of Freedom' by the Byrds. We pull up on a secluded peninsula, where Scott passes me a pre-rolled joint and a Zippo lighter.

'Fire up this doobie, dude.'

It is pure cannabis rolled in a thin white cigarette paper. Here, weed is plentiful enough to smoke it neat. Similar to a cigar, I rotate the torpedo-shaped joint between my thumb and index finger. Putting it in my mouth, I fire the lighter, hold the flame to the twisted paper tip and inhale the liquorice-tasting smoke.

'God made the world in six days,' Scott says as the car fills with smoke. 'On the seventh, he smoked Panama Red and said Far out!'

'And we're about to buy lots of it,' Jerry says, turning down a toke.

A smile crosses my face as the rush of sinsemilla overwhelms my power of reason.

'Think we should invest?' Jerry asks.

'Hell, yeah!' The crook inside my head replies.

***

Around midnight, Scott drops us off a safe distance from the mooring. Both of us gaze down at the ten bricks of compressed weed we snagged at $50 each. I'm stuck pot-rich and cash-poor until Jerry's paid and kicks back his half of the deal.

'How do we move all this on board without alerting the whole marina?' I inquire. 'We're practically guaranteed to wake someone up. We'll look like a couple of hod carriers.'

'Ah, the smuggler's dilemma,' Jerry muses, relishing the challenge. 'Figuring out how to hide something large enough not to miss.'

'The trick is to hide it in plain sight,' I say. Jerry looks at me.

'What, stack them on a bookshelf?'

'Well, if we only had one brick, I bet you could pull it off.'

'But we've ten. It'd be as thick as the Encyclopedia Britannica.'

'Or the Encyclopedia Botanica in this case.'

'Are you still stoned?'.

'Told you it's good weed. You should try some.'

'I never touch the merchandise.'

'You don't get high on your supply?'

'Never! I'm a professional.'

Realizing I'm too baked to come up with anything practical, I ask him what our move should be.

'The count's ordered me to change the engine oil tomorrow. It'll take time, as I'll have to pump it out by hand. While at it, I can stash the weed in the bilge under the oil pans. All you have to do is ensure no one sees me bringing these on board by creating a diversion.'

Digging with my hands, I bury the bricks in the sand while Jerry keeps watch. Then we slink back to the boat, our movements as furtive as grave robbers. Climbing on board, all is serene until Lucie stirs from under a blanket.

'An all-night party, huh?' she remarks.

'What's it to you?' Jerry retorts. 'We're grown men.'

She recoils at his abruptness. 'I was worried.'

With a shoulder shrug, Jerry vanishes below. I'm not able to get away so fast. Lucie tucks her legs up on the bench. 'Tell me all about the party?'

Sitting down, I spin her a tale about music and dancing.

'Sounds fun. A bit unfair though. You could have taken us with you.' Lucie unwraps herself from the blanket. 'You're wasted. Go to bed.' With her curt tone haunting me, I go below.

Lying in the Coffin, I kick myself. This trip is supposed to be a new start, a chance to leave deceit behind. Yet, by lying to cover up our shady dealings, nothing's changed. While Jerry will sleep soundly, I am haunted by guilt, betrayal, and deception while being chased by an ominous shadow through the labyrinthine corridors of the boat.

***

The lie expands over breakfast. The so-called party was at a nightclub with a live band playing great songs, including a killer cover of *Rikki Don't Lose That Number*. In short, I paint a picture of a Zonian utopia where kids attend dances, cruise in cool cars, revel in great music, and run wild.

'It's all right for some,' Johanna huffs. 'Next time, we're coming.'

'Yeah, where's this club?' Lucie inquires. 'Let's go tonight.'

'Enough of this talking,' Anna interjects, eager to finish the chores. 'I've got to use the laundry room. There's a mountain of things to wash. You girls are getting through your knickers…'

'What, at a rate of knots?' Arno jokes.

Anna shoots him an old-fashioned look as he gathers documents for the assaying department to calculate *Hoop*'s fee for transiting the Canal. Johanna and Lucie go off to find a payphone to connect with friends, leaving only Mickie to divert because, if given the chance, she'd want to help Jerry.

To buy him time, we could try to catch a monkey to keep as a pet, as pirates did back in the day. We're away for an hour, having fun, but were not 'softly, softly' enough to 'catchee monkey'. Although we did hear them chattering in the trees. Mickie, however, is clever enough to hustle me for an ice cream sundae.

Jerry finishes both jobs when Arno returns with the 'permission to transit' and orders to move to a holding anchorage, where we'll spend the night before going through the Canal tomorrow. Once everyone else is back on board, we motor off to pick up a mooring buoy. It's dark when we're secure for the night. Jerry and I cement our partnership with a drink.

'Hey, dude,' I say, handing him a beer, now content that we've gotten away with the first stage of our 'plan,' ignoring the fact that we're now criminals putting innocent people in jeopardy. 'Dick and Harry sounded sweet.' We clink bottles and take a gulp. 'Always remember the catchphrase: Trust your stash.'

'And you remember the other one,' he says, wiping his mouth with the back of his hand. 'Loose talk costs lives.'

This morning, I'm woken up by the intense and terrifying screams of howler monkeys warning each other of the dangers of the day. Coffee cup in hand, I climb out of the hatch when a snub-nosed launch bounces against us, making me spill half of it.

'That's a poor start to your day,' the pilot says, jumping on board as a green cloud of noisy parakeets fly by in tight formation. 'But if you're making another one, milk and two sugars for me.'

He is a lively, light-haired man with a face blotched with keratosis scars, a testament to a life in the tropics. I hand him my half-full mug, which he takes with a nod while pointing out that I'm to help take on board six tyres for use as fenders and four stout 125-foot hawsers necessary for the passage through the Canal.

When his walkie-talkie bursts into life in a crackle of static, the pilot tells us it's time to leave. It's quickly turning into one of those days as I mop up the spillage while Arno starts the engines and Jerry casts off. Squeezing out a rag over the side, I feel *Hoop* head off towards the first of three sequential locks that will lift us ninety feet to Gatun Lake.

With the girls now on deck, the pilot guides us through the gaping mouth of towering lock gates. We glide slowly into a vast concrete space enclosed by thirty-foot-high, rough-cast walls. With fenders out to protect her flanks, Arno stops behind our transit buddy, a colossal freighter registered in Mauritania; a place I didn't realize existed outside Marx Brothers films.

A mighty clang echoes around the chamber as the lock gates close behind us. Now floating on an unctuous brew of oil slick and debris, *Hoop* feels tiny and insignificant next to such a large ship. With no way out of here but up, I'm overcome by a sense of claustrophobia but keen to put on a good show.

Our first job is to hoist four lock lines up to *las mulas*, the Panamanian line handlers way above us. With each line over a hundred feet long, the deck's a sea of rope, and we must pay attention at every turn. I learn the hard way what a lapse in concentration means. The line handlers throw leather-bound weights on the end of thin messenger lines. We are then to tie these to the heavy lock lines. I watch, fascinated, as one man spins the *bolas* before propelling it towards our stern with the speed and precision of a slingshot. Jerry catches it and deftly ties on our line, which is hauled up and secured to a dockside bollard. While admiring this skill, the monkey-fist-sized weight I'm supposed to catch slams into my left buttock with a force that almost topples me. Peals of laughter from the workers above echo around the chasm as I hop along the deck, clutching my arse.

'You've made someone's day,' our pilot shouts. 'Idiots like you are hard to find.'

According to his orders, we keep *Hoop* centred inside the lock by tightening the lines as the sluices open and water rushes in. Deflected by the ship in front, a current surge creates a whirlpool that makes it hard to keep us from spinning out of control. Once conditions stabilize, the water gently raises us to the next level, and the second lock looms ahead. When the tall metal gates open, another chasm towers above us—its dripping, moss-covered walls torn with enormous impact scars. Arno is the most anxious I've seen him, and no wonder. We are as vulnerable as a matchbox in a trucker's backside pocket.

When the rear doors seal shut, a klaxon blasts, and the water rises again. The incoming flood puts so much pressure on a stern line that it snaps, and we spin towards the lock wall. There's a mighty thud as Lucie's fender flattens against the rub-rail. She reaches out to protect *Hoop* from the impact. I grab her waist and pull her back. Luckily, the bumper does its job, and we swing back into the middle of the lock as the swell subsides.

Indifferent that Lucie could have been injured, the pilot shouts to her that, 'God made women's arms to embrace men, not fight walls.' Infuriated by his crass remark, she shakes me off, walking away as though the moment never happened.

Similar to Orpheus in a Greek tragedy, we slowly ascend from the underworld to reach the top of the second lock. Here, the relaxed attitude of the Canal workers going about their daily business, talking to each other in a series of coded whistles, makes light of our foolish anxiety. Oblivious to the stress of those transiting for the first time, their 'couldn't care less' attitude is the price we pay for not going around Cape Horn.

The ship in front moves off, and we follow it into Lake Gatun, the artificial reservoir trapped between locks at each end of the Canal.

Disembarking the pilot, we learn our transit is delayed as a US Naval asset is passing through under cover of darkness.

We are to keep out of the way and spend the night tied to a buoy in calm water out of the main channel. *Hoop* is now eighty-five feet above the level of the Caribbean Sea where we started this morning.

***

Stuck in the sweltering tropical heat with time on our hands, Anna makes a practical suggestion.

'*Meine Kinder!*' she says, letting down the swimming ladder, 'Wash off the sweat or the mosquitoes will feast on our *Fleisch*.'

Johanna and Lucie strip off on deck and leap into the water. I follow suit, relishing a midnight swim in broad daylight.

'Geronimo!' shouts Mickie as she dive-bombs us from the rigging, creating such a splash that it soaks Jerry, who's left standing on the deck, looking bemused by the pile of clothes at his feet. After Arno takes an elegant dive off the transom and Anna lowers herself in clutching a beach ball, Jerry is like a lonely cloud on a sunny day as we all swim around the boat Garden-of-Eden naked. Johanna is the first to tease him, and we all join in, but he's adamant about not getting his kit off, so he jumps in with his shorts on.

Playing piggy in the middle, we thrash about, utterly abandoned to sheer joy. It turns physical as the Camaris clan are all strong swimmers who take no prisoners. I come under sustained attack when we grab the ball.

When the fun's over, a sudden burst of modesty makes me

reluctant to leave the water. Never one to miss an opportunity to put idle hands working, Anna passes me a face mask, snorkel and knife so I can scrape off any barnacle beards from the hull. In the cool water, it's a pleasant enough task. When Arno comes to inspect the keel, I take one glimpse at his speargun and figure it's time to get out.

***

Twilight doesn't happen at this latitude. Darkness falls at once, after sunset. The raucous sounds of the jungle cease, and the sweet-scented flowers close for the night, leaving just the croaking of frogs and a pungent smell of rotting vegetation to fill the air.

While Arno and Anna bicker in German down below, the rest of us sit in the cockpit with the warm, wet air sitting thick on our tongues. The game of Pontoon we play to pass the time after supper loses its charm when Jerry loses his stake to Mickie—the banker.

'You're cheating,' he says as the little tyke scoops up his stake.

'Bad losers always bitch. Get over it,' Mickie says with a forcefulness that shocks us all.

Sensing that Jerry might take offense, even though we're only playing for tokens, I throw in my hand and tell Mickie it's time to go to bed. Taking her winnings, she leaves, followed shortly by Johanna and Lucie.

Jerry and I stay in the cockpit and crack another warm beer. Wanting to find out more about his time in the army, I ask him what happened after he took the Queen's shilling.

'The military is part of the government, and governments are stupid. So doing your duty means doing stupid stuff.'

When I ask what he means, he says the politicians panicked when the British pulled out of Aden in '67 and left vehicles, tons of ammo and comms equipment behind.

'Guess what the last job they ordered me to do was?'

'Destroy the runway?'

'No! I told you governments are stupid. I had to blow up the garrison beer ration—all fifty thousand bottles.'

'Why?'

'In case the locals took offense at us leaving alcohol behind.' For a moment he has the faraway eyes of someone remembering something forgotten. 'Boom!' He simulates an explosion with his hands. 'I saw grown men cry at the sight of it. The place must have stunk like a brewery for months.'

My mind boggles at the thought as I finish my beer. 'What did the army teach you then?'

'What every squaddie learns on day one and knows to be true until the day they leave: If it moves, salute it. If it doesn't, paint it; if no one is looking, steal it.'

'Did you know what you wanted to do when you left?' I ask him as Arno comes up on deck to join us.

'No, but not in a million years did I imagine I'd be here now,' Jerry says by way of nothing.

'Well, you can't be anywhere else but here,' the captain says as though we're idiots. 'It's not logical to think otherwise.'

We sit listening to the frogs until a low rumbling sound of well-oiled gears, shafts and rotating propellers drowns them out. Against the lights on the opposite bank, the silhouettes of the five-inch guns make the US Navy destroyer's ghostly progress even more ominous.

'They're moving her through at night to avoid upsetting the Panamanians,' Arno says. 'They want the Canal back, and with the place at fever pitch, an American warship in the middle of their country might spark more riots.'

After the others have sloped off to bed, I sit on the swimming ladder so my toes can dip in the water. With my legs straddling two oceans, I savour the last of my beer and toss the empty bottle into the water. While it gurgles to the bottom, I realize it's not a metaphor I'm living; I am at a crossroads. Looking up at the stars, the Southern Cross heralds an unfamiliar world. It's starting a new journey, with all the fear of the unknown. If I knew what to ask for, I'd make a wish.

***

The following morning in the blue hour before sunrise, and with the early-bird chorus echoing through the jungle, Arno, Jerry and I are up before the others to prepare for the thirty-seven-mile passage ahead of us. I make coffee while Jerry warms up the engines, and Arno goes on the two-way radio and calls in. 'Cristobal Signal Station, this is the sailing vessel *Hoop*, Hotel Oscar Oscar Papa,' he growls in his thick, early-morning voice, telling the port authorities we're up.

In the muted glow of the first light, a new pilot arrives by harbour taxi to shepherd us along the misty ribbon of water cutting through the hills ahead. Younger than yesterday's old hand, he jumps on board, a new Panama Canal Pilot Association patch on his jacket.

Caffeine-fed, I head to the prow, awaiting the order to slip our mooring and shift from one ocean to another. For me it's a pivot point. We're moving from the Atlantic, where I learned the sailor's trade, to the Pacific and embarking on the other great maritime tradition—smuggling.

'Let go of the bow line,' Arno bellows. We reverse away from the buoy. *Hoop* shudders into forward gear, and we head out into a sudden tropical downpour. It's the first I've experienced outside, and though the cloudburst passes as quickly as it came, I'm soaked.

'It is your rain tax,' the pilot laughs. 'We need it to replenish what we lose in every transit.'

'Thirty-two million gallons,' Arno adds.

My job is put on hold since we must motor at a constant speed of four knots, with no sailing permitted. Leaving Arno to converse with the pilot and Jerry content at the helm, I change my wet clothes below. Down in the galley, Anna's making breakfast, so I hang around hoping for a tidbit.

'It must be nice to have a stove that keeps still for once,' I remark, sensing how calm our passage is now without the swell that makes cooking on a gimbaled hob such a challenge.

'Yes, but just because it's smooth on the surface doesn't mean no restlessness underneath.'

The remark takes me aback, as talking in riddles is unlike Anna. I wonder if she's apprehensive about entering the Pacific. 'Aren't you glad you're on the right side of the globe to return to Vancouver?'

She turns the bacon in the skillet and sighs. 'Living in such close quarters can expose a marriage's shortcomings,' she says. It occurs to me that I may be the first non-family member that Anna has had a chance to talk to in a while. Although I'm not the best listener, she finds comfort in confiding in me while she fries her eggs. 'And once the cat's out of the bag,' she butters a muffin, 'it won't go back in.'

'Why are you two talking about cats?' Johanna asks, coming in and snaffling the rasher of bacon I've been eyeing up, earning her a slap with the spatula from Anna.

'We had one my last boat who loved pork,' I say, deflecting the focus away from Anna, who has a tear in her eye.

'What's not to like?' Johanna says, sitting at the table and licking her fingers. 'I'm starving.'

Shrugging her shoulder, Anna hands me an egg and bacon muffin. Our moment of confidence is over for now; I think we're allies.

***

Like a lucky monkey, I climb the ratlines to eat my breakfast in peace and enjoy a ride over water so glassy I can see our reflection. Sitting up here in the rigging, I hope to spot a blue-footed booby. Not that I'm an avid birdwatcher, but I'm taken by the name and want to see what a booby looks like, blue feet or not. I don't spot one, but along the shoreline are colonies of brown pelicans nesting in the lush vegetation. They make low-pitched croaks at each other while sitting on scrappy-looking nests. Then, as though one has given an order, a flock lifts off in formation to plunge-dive and prey on fish—impervious to the ships moving about.

Interrupting my birding moment, Lucie climbs up and grabs my hand, and takes a bite of my muffin. 'My, that tastes good.'

'Other people's food always does.'

The wash from a ship jostles us; we link arms to steady each other.

'You're a strange creature. What are you doing up here all alone?'

'Trying to work out where these ships are heading.'

'They're so big here but only specks on the horizon at sea.'

'That's because they're far away. It's all a matter of perspective.' I josh her, reckoning she's easily teased.

'Check that one out.' She points to a floating crane moving along in the procession of ships. 'It's gigantic.'

'That's because it's close up.'

The remark earns me a nudge in the ribs.

The crane passes us in the opposite direction. The name 'Hercules' is inscribed along its flank.

'Who was Hercules?' Lucie asks.

'Son of Zeus. A super strong Roman god.'

'Okay Poindexter! Didn't he carry the world on his shoulders?'

'No, that was Atlas. It's why maps in a book are called an Atlas.'

The wisecrack gets me another nudge to say—stop that nonsense.

'It's awesome to hang out with someone who makes me laugh.'

'Snap!' I reply, wondering if it's a friendly gesture or flirtatious one.

'Oh, my god! Look at that!' Shrieking, Lucie points to a nine-foot crocodile moving alongside us. 'It might have eaten us yesterday.'

'All stark-naked,' I reply with a comic leer in my voice.

'You're not supposed to think like that,' she says, taking me as literally as her father. 'Like it's dirty. We're of Germanic stock and have a healthy attitude to our bodies. Naked is natural.'

My defense mechanism jumps in. 'I didn't mean it that way.'

'Brits are so repressed!' she says exasperated.

Trying to recover lost ground, I make light of the situation. 'A boatload of bare bums is not a regular sight.'

'Bums! Pah! Boobs! Yawn! In the Mediterranean, you can't move for tits and dicks waving around in the wind.'

Grasping that I'm not dealing with an average person, I change the subject. 'You're such a bohemian.'

'Of course! Papa's a real one, from Bohemia!'

'What is his background? I'm a tad confused.'

Oh, that's simple. He's a naturalized Canadian citizen of Austrian birth from a noble family harking back to the Austro/Hungarian Empire with ancestral lands in Bohemia, now part of Czechoslovakia.

'It's in the blood then?'

'Yes, blue blood, and, at last, we can let the world know.

'Have you been waiting for something?'

'Papa has finally allowed us to use the title of Countess. He forbade it for years, saying we were too poor. Then, when we picked up *Hoop* in the Baltic, he started calling himself 'Count.' I'm not sure what's changed, but something has.'

'It's useful when you're arriving in strange places. Sets you apart.'

'And taking your kids out of school, floating them around the world for a year—that isn't enough? We're like a travelling circus.'

'How does it feel now that you're heading home?'

'I'm worried about going back to college,' she pauses, her voice tinged with uncertainty. 'I'm not sure I'll fit in.'

Around us, I can hear the whine of mosquitoes gathering.

'Surely, the guys will see you as a heroine of the high seas. You'll be the campus champ.'

She scoffs lightly, brushing off my attempt at comfort. 'I intimidate them as it is. They get tongue-tied and talk utter gibberish.'

'Why? You're not that overwhelming.'

'Thanks for the backhanded compliment, but I'll cash in on a genuine one if one's going. I'll even give you a discount.'

A giant mosquito lands on her bare arm. I brush it off with a smile. 'Okay, okay. You are an elusive prize, a tantalizing dream beyond their grasp.'

'What do you mean elusive?' There's playfulness in her voice.

'Aloof, mysterious. That 'look but don't touch' vibe.'

'But you just touched me!' She points out grinning.

'Yes, but I'm not a teenager.'

'No, but you're a fairy so it doesn't count.'

'I'm a mosquito slayer, immune to your intimidation tactics.'

She laughs. 'Oh, so now I have intimidation tactics?'

'Absolutely. You've got that '*I'm too cool for you*' thing going on. It's quite the strategy.'

'Thanks for the analysis. I'll be sure to use my powers for good, not evil.'

'Remember, with great power comes great responsibility.'

'Don't worry, I won't let it go to my head. Or should I?'

Squishing a giant mosquito feeding on my leg, I feel the blood dribble down my thigh.

'Time to go in, or we'll be bitten to death.'

***

When we reach the Gaillard Cut, it's my turn at the helm, but all I can see are the scars of hand-hewn rock in the steep-sided banks. With an earthy smell on the hot wind blowing through the pass and the quality of light changing, it may be a foretaste of what lies ahead. The eight-mile channel dug out of the continental divide is one of *the* engineering feats of the turn of the century, achieved in part by the deaths of countless workers carted away daily like fallen timber.

With the others all below, leaving only the pilot and me on watch, it becomes monotonous. Ships pass us coming the other way, but no one is on deck even to wave at. We bounce in their wake as trivial as a rubber duck in a bath. The rain returns, and the pilot takes cover. Left alone, I daydream of owning a boat, circling the globe, living at sea, and even wondering if Lucie would come along. I'd call our boat *Forever Young*, as right now, life is juicy. I feel at my peak.

When Arno comes to relieve me, I search for the pilot. For a moment, I'm convinced he's joined those sailors found drowned with their zippers undone, having fallen overboard when taking a pee, but I find him napping under a tarp. 'Coca-Cola,' he mutters as I prod him awake, but we've none on board.

The first pair of locks on the Pacific side of the Canal are at Pedro Miguel, three-quarters of a mile upstream from the last two at Miraflores. These are here so if one fails, all the water from Gatun Lake doesn't drain into the ocean.

After passing through the locks and disembarking the pilot with a fat tip, we approach the Bridge of the Americas that connects the two continents. It's over a mile long and tall enough for large ships to pass under at high tide. Arno calls me to examine the radar.

'What do you make of this?' he says, pointing at the scanner, which shows a straight line across our path. In the dark, it would have appeared as a solid wall, and I'd have panicked, but as we approach the bridge, the line opens like a magic door before slamming shut as we pass under the highway far above our heads.

'It only applies to bridges. Don't try it with a breakwater.'

Although the Canal is impressive, leaving it behind is a relief, and now we're out of the shipping lane. I walk up the deck to Lucie, who's come out to watch the sunset on a new horizon.

'Hello Océano Pacífico, the peaceful ocean,' I say, stretching out my arms as if to embrace it. 'A new sea for you to conquer.'

'You're such a poet.' Her mouth curves smiling. 'Tell me more.'

'Well, little Miss Lay-a-bed.' I declaim in thespian exaggeration,

'Ah, the splendor of the Atlantic dawn, akin to the bloom of morning glory! But as the sun casts its final rays upon the ocean's edge, we bid farewell to the radiant god Helios, who, with a petit mort, falls spent into the embrace of Pacific dusk.'

While the last rays of red and orange sunlight spread across the water, she grabs me by my shirt. 'OK, Oscar Wilde. But if you think you are going ashore tonight to have fun without me, you'll never see the sun rise again.'

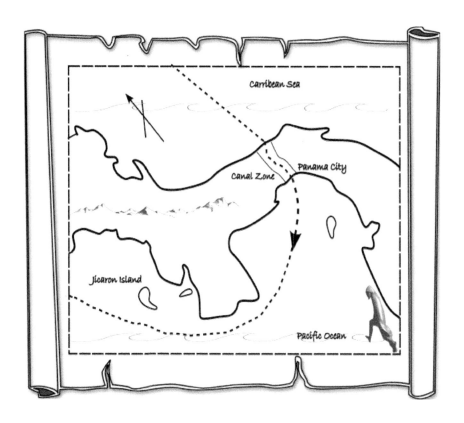

Chapter 3

Blood Stains

Before heading to Hawaii tomorrow, we refuel and pick up a swing mooring so *Hoop* can move freely, as the tidal range here averages twelve feet, and the current is strong. Even though the yacht club at the end of the long pier looks rundown, it's where the count wants us to eat and take an early night. But the girls have other plans.

Although Balboa is in the American-controlled zone, it's a suburb of Panama City, which ranks along with New York as one of the world's most dangerous places. Be that as it may, the girls bully their parents into letting them go out for the evening if Jerry and I take responsibility—a commitment I have doubts about.

'And don't wake us when you come back,' Arno adds, tickling Mickie, who's also indignant at not being allowed to go. 'We have a lot to do before setting off.'

We're soon ready for a night of fun. Jerry is wearing slacks and a European Cup Final T-shirt, while I am dressed in a linen suit to match the girls' skimpy dresses. We board the dinghy unnoticed by the 'rents' and head ashore, then make our way to Fourth of July Avenue, which marks the perimeter of the Canal Zone. Here, the contrast is stark between a well-ordered US territory and a banana republic, where bored, edgy paramilitary soldiers patrol the streets.

'In Panama City,' the Zonian police officer says to Jerry as we wait to cross the road, 'the only rule is there ain't no rules.' He tips the brim of his blue Stetson cavalry hat, and his hand eases down to rest on the butt of a stainless-steel Smith & Wesson Magnum revolver. 'Y'all take care over there because I can't come to rescue you.'

The cop has no sooner spoken than the girls, heedless of his advice, set off across the road.

'Hey, no jaywalking,' he shouts after them.

'I thought there weren't any rules,' Johanna yells back.

Aware we're up for a run-around, I set off in hot pursuit, leaving Jerry talking to the cop. He catches up with me along Harrison Avenue, where the girls are already attracting attention. A small gang of guys, all pimped up for the night, gawk and whistle while Johanna and Lucie preen themselves.

'Where are you going to take us?' Johanna asks Jerry, all sassy-like.

Without skipping a beat, he confidently guides us down a bustling street filled with a mix of battered American cars, bicycles, motor scooters, and colourful buses. The constant noise of horns honking and beeping echoes up and down the road as drivers deal with the one thing that matters—don't hit anything in front.

Jerry turns right and jostles through a crowd onto Casco Viejo, where the smell of fried plantains and sweet coconut lingers on the warm night air. He heads us down a narrow street of elegant colonial buildings tucked inside the centuries-old city walls. Everywhere, we pass bars and brothels open to restless newcomers seeking another raucous night. Jerry stops us outside one cool-looking venue.

'How did you find out about this place?' I ask.

'I asked the cop while you lot were jaywalking.'

'And you took it all in?'

'Soldiers listen to orders. Lives depend on it.'

Impatient, Johanna interrupts, 'I want a drink.'

***

Inside, it's a cauldron of energy with heads swinging in screw-faced joy to percussive Latin rhythms. The Panamanians are a good-looking, loose-hipped race, and they know it.

'Now listen,' Jerry says, coming over all parentals. 'This place is full of modern-day marauders. Keep your traps shut about where you've been and where we're going.'

'Yeah, yeah, yeah!' Johanna's tone is defiant as usual. 'We weren't born yesterday.'

I laugh at her. She gives me a withering look, her almond eyes blazing with indignation.

'Oh Johanna, you're so sweet when you're angry.'

'Sweet! Sweet!' she shoots back, fizzing like a firework. 'I'm not bloody sweet. If you think I'm sweet, you can go hang. Come on, Lucie, let's find some real men.'

'Good riddance,' Jerry waves them away with his hand.

The girls slide onto the dance floor as one. Seeing how they effortlessly find willing dance partners is frustrating, making my rejection as a contender even more annoying. They shimmy across the dance floor, enjoying themselves, I feel jealous and left on the sidelines as a spectator.

Jerry snaps me back to reality. 'Forget them. Let's get drunk.'

We start the night with bottles of icy Balboa beer, a refreshing gnat-piss we turn into a chaser by drinking it with local rum. With sailors' abandon we're well on the way when a woman Jerry's been giving the eye comes over to flirt with him.

Given my experience in Puerto Rico, I reckon she's probably drugged-up *travesti*. 'She's a hooker,' I whisper. '*una mariposa.*'

'Well, get you. You and your boy scout badge for the bleeding obvious.' Jerry's all pumped up and eager to go. 'Why do you think I brought us here? I asked the cop for a blow bar.'

Leaning over, the woman points to a semi-private booth and holds up two fingers to show the price in dollars for services. Jerry nods in my direction and says, 'His barrel's bent, but I shoot straight.' With that cute remark, he hops off with his hot Latina.

Sitting with my drink. Uncomfortable in the heat, I keep my eye on the girls, who are now ensconced with a couple of guys at a table. Johanna is babbling away in full flow. Lucie ignores my glance in the way a child hides behind their hands, thinking you can't see them. I want to be dancing with her, but sit inept, my feet tapping the floor in frustration. Jerry's trick doesn't take long. He comes back smiling.

'How was it?'

'She made five minutes feel like twenty. Gave me a bloody brilliant blow job. I shot my load. She swallowed, all for two bucks.' He knocks back a rum. 'Result!'

'She's a transvestite,' I tease him. 'Who's the homo now?'

'What?' Jerry splutters into his glass. 'A chick with a dick?' He laughs. 'Any port in a storm, mate. But not a word about it to anyone.' He finishes his drink. 'Get the girls. We're heading back.'

Jerry stumbles and bumps into someone as he makes for the door, which prompts an exchange of insults. Steering well clear, I head to the table where two lotharios are beguiling the girls with Latin charm.

'Sorry to break this up,' I say. 'but we've got to go back.'

'Don't be such a wet blanket.' Johanna gives me a contemptuous glare. 'You sound like a teacher.'

The two guys are indignant, making it clear with hand gestures.

'I'm serious! Jerry's fighting drunk. We've got to go.'

'We're having fun,' Lucie says. 'Can't we stay longer?'

'No! Out now!' My words carry the weight of an elder brother's authority. To my relief, Lucie rises from her seat, and even the reluctant Johanna follows suit. Sensing trouble on the horizon, the two guys raise their arms in submission.

'Goodbye, contessa,' a pock-marked-faced guy says to Johanna. 'You must invite me to visit your boat.'

She dismisses his advance with a wave. 'We're leaving at dawn.'

'What else did you tell him?'

'Nothing much; he loves boats and asked where we are moored.'

'And you're a countess,' I say, emphasizing the title with air quotes.

'Well, I am!' Johanna retorts, her tone arch. 'What's the point in lying? It impresses people and they think we're rich.'

'Two for the price of one.' A sozzled Lucie jokes.

'Johanna, you're right!' I say, ushering them towards the door. 'I was wrong! You're not sweet. You're stupid!'

The taxi's bodywork is full of dings and dents. The old Pontiac seems like it's survived fire and robbery, but it bounces along just fine. A furry football dangles where a rearview mirror should be, and the girls squeal as we jerk from side to side. The cabbie takes us on a white-knuckle ride. Sitting in the front, I face the full force of the driver's love for Panama and loathing of America, feelings he makes clear with staccato hand gestures and emphatic honks of the horn.

'Tell him to shut the fuck up,' Jerry slurs, slumped in the back. He carries on about what a shithole the place is.

'Oh, be a gentleman for once,' I say, turning round to face him, 'and not some lowlife, pissed-up squaddie.'

My remark brings an uncomfortable silence. The girls stare intently out their windows.

'You're going to regret saying that.' Jerry man-spreads his legs. 'Not today, not tomorrow, but one day you'll wish you'd kept your trap shut.' We drive on, uptight and uncomfortable in the heat, with Lucie's hiccups punctuating the awkwardness.

Back at the yacht club pontoon, I we squeeze into the tender. It's colder on the water. The girls begin to shiver. I row out to *Hoop* with a will. The moon is rising, so I don't need her anchor light to guide me to the boarding ladder. Once on deck, Johanna slips off to bed without saying a word.

After taking a piss over the side, Jerry stumbles to his bunk, the worse for wear; I was wrong to have baited him and regret calling him a squaddie. It was a silly piece of public-school twattery so I could show off to the girls and pretend I was in their class. As if!

'Thanks for getting us back, Plum Bum,' Lucie says, hiccups over.

'I suppose I'm stuck with that nickname.'

'Yes,' She pecks me on the cheek. 'I think it's sweet.'

Wriggling into the Coffin as I now call my quarters, it's too hot for the sleeping bag, so lie on top in cutoffs and a T-shirt. Lucie comes to mind. I picture her sailing with her hair blowing in the wind and chuckle at her attempt at humor. I can't deny a growing fascination.

During the night, I am pulled out of a dream and thrown into the present. My curiosity is sparked as *Hoop* tilts slightly, only to correct herself. It isn't a sway caused by the wake of a passing boat, and with no tell-tale splash, it's not Jerry's drunken misstep overboard. Intrigued, I get up to investigate.

Stepping out of the companionway hatch, a man stands three feet away with a gun leveled at my head. An accomplice brandishes a machete, casting an ominous shadow over the unfolding nightmare.

'What the fuck do you want?' I shout, desperation lacing my voice, hoping it will alert the others.

'Shut up, or you die!' snaps the guy, focusing the revolver on my face. In a second, I recognize the pockmarked punk from the bar.

'You!'

'Yes, we meet again. Now, give us the money.'

'We don't have any money,' I stammer, my legs trembling.

'You gringos have dollars.' He spits the words in a hot gust of air.

'You have thousands of dollars on board.' His accomplice joins in. 'We'll kill you if we don't get the money—NOW!'

The aft cabin door opens, spilling light on the scene, and Jerry appears bleary-eyed. 'What the fuck?' he exclaims, taking it in. Sobering up fast, he slams the cabin door shut, shouting to the girls, 'We're being robbed. Stay inside and lock the door.'

The man with the machete seizes him, forcefully pushing him into the cockpit with the side of the blade. 'Shut up and join your friend.'

'We don't have any money,' I repeat, my legs shaking as I lift an arm in defense.

'You gringos all have dollars.' His flying spittle rains on my face.

'It's the owner you want, not us,' Jerry interjects, his voice flat and matter of fact, as though he's detached from the gravity of the situation. 'He has lots of dollars.'

The pockmarked guy points the gun toward the forward companionway. 'You two get below. Don't try anything, or the countess gets cut!'

Pushed from behind, we pile into the saloon on top of each other. The guy lurks in the hatchway, signaling with his gun for us to move.

'What the hell is going on?' Arno shouts, appearing from his cabin, furious at being woken up.

'We're being robbed,' Jerry says, pointing out the gunman, half hidden in the dark. 'They want money.'

Arno lurches forward, but Jerry stops him with the flat of his hand. 'There are two of them. The other's up by the aft cabin with a machete.' Arno stares at him in disbelief. 'The girls are safe for now. They're locked in.'

'These guys were chatting up the girls last night,' I blurt out. 'They think we have money on board.'

'Always showing off,' Arno mutters, his words laced with anger.

'Hey, quit talking. Give me the cash.'

Arno slumps down on a settee. 'There isn't any.'

The guy laughs. He knows better. 'Don't lie to me. The contessa tells me how rich you are!'

'I thought you were supposed to be looking after them,' Arno growls at Jerry and me.

'*Que Passa?*' the machete man shouts down. '*Vamos!*'

'Give me the money quick!' his partner shouts at Arno in a breathy explosion of desperation. '*Mucha plata rápidamente!*'

The side stateroom door opens, and Mickie runs in.

'Papa, what's all the noise?' She stops, then cries.'

'Shut the fuck up!' The guy waves his pistol at her.

Arno pulls Mickie close to him. 'In that drawer, that's all the cash there is,' he says, his voice indignant, his eyes furious.

The gunman wrinkles his nose at me. 'Get it, blondie.' The tension tightens as the demand intensifies.

In zombie mode, I head to the chart table and pull out a fistful of dollar bills. Then something clicks. The guy's pint-sized; I can grab the gun and overpower him. Adrenaline floods my veins. I turn around, fearless. But before I make any move, Jerry senses the sudden bravado. He snatches the cash with one hand and punches me in the stomach with the other. The impact ripples through my body. Winded, I collapse to the floor. The gunman, agitated, points the pistol at everyone. Arno pulls Mickie's close. 'Come here, my *pumpernickel*. You're safe with Papa.'

Jerry offers the wad of cash. 'Here, take it. It's over three hundred.'

The gunman snatches the dollar bills. '*Coño,*' He wipes his mouth with the back of his hand. '*Coño.*' Hundreds are not what he came for, not enough to make the risk worthwhile. He's after thousands.

¿Que pasó? his accomplice shouts. *¿Que pasó loco?*

The tension is palpable as the gunman hesitates. Jerry fills the void.

'This is nothing,' he says, looking at the money with disdain. His voice assumes a different tone as he whispers a betrayal. 'Like you said, more money must be hidden on the boat.'

'Get it now!' the gunman orders, his nervous eyes darting around.

'Take the cash.' Come a shout from above. '*Vámonos!* Let's go!'

I try to stand up, Jerry kicks my hand from under me. Unafraid he leans toward the gunman. 'I hate these people,' he whispers, as though sharing an intimacy. 'They pay me nothing.' He pauses. 'I've a plan for you to get rich.' The room is tense as Jerry hints at his hidden agenda. 'I'll help you steal the yacht. We'll find the money later. You take the dollars. I take the boat.' A flicker of a smile crosses the gunman's lips. Jerry presses on. 'If we go now, no one will notice.' He adds as a bonus, 'And you have fun with the girls.'

'Son of a bitch,' I spit, still prone on the floor. Jerry kicks me hard.

The guy with the gun shouts up to his friend, and they exchange words in staccato Panamanian. 'It's a fast ship,' Jerry says, hustling them into a decision. 'We could use it to smuggle drugs.'

'OK, gringo,' the gunman says, his greed inflamed. 'Do anything crazy, and I'll kill you.' He then backs out of the companionway. Jerry follows him to the cockpit and closes the hatch, locking us below.

**

Struggling to my feet, I appeal to Arno. 'What are we to do?'

'Wait here! Jerry is a dead man.' He takes Mickie to Anna, still hidden behind the stateroom door.

The sound of the engines starting reverberates around the boat. Trapped in the saloon and overwhelmed by a sense of helplessness, I yell at Jerry in defiance. My words are ignored by the excited talk in the cockpit as someone goes forward to cut the mooring line.

Diesel fumes seep into the cabin as *Hoop* goes into reverse. With my heart beating fast, I grab the cook's knife from the galley. Then, without warning, the engines go full tilt ahead, and we swerve this way and that. As we spin out of control, pans fly, and the girls scream riding a fairground ride from hell. The chaos intensifies, each moment adding to the frantic pace of the unfolding disaster.

Next, *Hoop* shudders as the gearbox slams into reverse. We stop short. I bang my head and drop the knife. The cabin fills with smoke. I cough. The hatch slides back.

'Plum!' Jerry shouts. 'Come up here quick.'

Crawling out onto the deck, I spot Jerry, his arm outstretched with a gun pointed at one of the men clinging to the rigging.

'Take over the helm.'

'Where's the other guy?'

'Back there somewhere,' Jerry says with a nod. 'He needed a swim and left his gun behind. Didn't want to get it wet, I guess.'

'Fuck, man, what went down?'

'Keep her steady,' Jerry says. 'But be ready to swerve. This guy's still got his machete and may make a run at us.'

It's then I notice blood on the wheel and realize I'm bleeding from the bash to my head. I can feel it running down my face and dripping off my chin. Gazing down the boat, I catch a fleeting shadow. Under the shroud lights, Arno emerges from the forehatch, speargun leveled at Jerry—and by consequence, me.

'Drop the gun,' he shouts, half hidden behind the mast. 'This is my boat. I've had everything taken away from me once. It won't happen again.' His voice is full of meaning and menace.

'Only when this punk drops his machete, skipper,' Jerry shouts back, pointing the pistol at the hapless stooge.

Realizing two trained killers are facing each other down, I play referee. 'It was all a charade,' I shout out, as though I've witnessed a miracle. 'Jerry played them for a pair of patsies.'

Taking advantage of the distraction, the pirate drops the blade on the deck, hurls himself over the side, and starts to swim away. Jerry follows the splashing with the barrel of the gun.

'Don't do it, mate,' I plead. 'It's not worth it.'

'Oh, it's mate now, is it?' he says, lowering the weapon. 'I wouldn't fire this piece of crap if you paid me.'

'Why not?'

'A Warsaw Pact 7.65mm automatic pistol, accurate to fifteen yards. Would the ammo be dependable in the tropics? Probably not. Click-bang, as we call it. You pull the trigger and peer down the barrel, wondering where the bullet has gone—not advisable.'

'Would the other guy have used it?'

'Doubt it. The punks were greedy, not killers. Their plan was half-baked. Pulling a trigger on someone is tricky if they're not shooting.'

'I don't believe in guns,' I reply, recalling when a gun exploded over my head as a warning on *Gay Gander*.

'You don't have to believe; simply point, squeeze, and watch in disbelief as you miss nine times out of ten.'

***

Jerry and I return *Hoop* to her mooring while Arno is on the two-way, making a distress call on Channel 16. He reports two men in the water and an attempted hijacking. While waiting for the Coast Guard to turn up, Jerry and I sit in the cockpit. He is distant and detached while I'm trying to calm down and work out what happened.

Notwithstanding the sticky mat of hair and congealing blood on my head, I couldn't have bled as much as the splatter stains around the cockpit show. Seeing Lucie come out of the cabin brings me up short.

'Oh, Plum,' she says, looking at my wound, 'you're such a hero helping save us all.'

For a moment, bathed in her warmth, I feel I'm one. Jerry sneers, 'If he's the man of your dreams, luv, you'd better wake up.'

Moments later, a high-speed patrol boat is heading toward us, its searchlight sweeping the water. The vessel comes alongside, a pair of machine guns in its bow turret, ominous and deadly in the faint light of a waning moon.

An officer of the Southern Coast Guard jumps on deck with the confidence of a man who only needs probable cause to board a vessel.

We gather in the saloon, where I blurt out an account of events, avoiding mentioning having met the robbers earlier and the girls spilling the beans about the boat's location. Then Jerry tells his side of the story, saying the gunman lost his footing and fell overboard as the boat sped out of control. While confirming the story but skirting over details, Arno adds that they forced Jerry into starting the engines as they were planning to hijack us.

'You're lucky to have an ex-soldier on board. This may have turned ugly. These guys were high on drugs and capable of anything.'

'Jerry was calm under fire,' Arno says.

'Oh, yes,' the officer says as if reminding himself. 'You can keep the popgun as a souvenir. But I'd better take the ammunition.'

Jerry slips out the magazine and empties the bullets from the clip. The officer counts them and smiles. 'I'll have the one up the spout.'

'Can't blame a man for trying,' Jerry says with a laugh, emptying the chamber. 'This is a rare caliber.'

'You won't find a slug to fit that between here and Tucumcari.'

'What happens now?' Jerry asks.

'The way it appears to me,' the officer conjectures, thinking aloud, 'if these punks make it back, rumors will spread, and they'll concoct some bullshit about them being the victims.'

'But they came out to rob us,' Arno insists firmly.

'Listen up, folks. It appears the thieves who targeted your boat were opportunists. Since your vessel is the largest in the harbour, they assumed it would be an easy mark and stole the canoe trailing off your stern from the beach. Unfortunately, this isn't the first time this has happened. In most cases, the victims pay up and move on.'

Arno's brow furrows. 'If you catch them, will we have to stay?'

The officer lifts his cap and scratches his buzz cut. 'Right now, At this moment, the Panamanian government is trying to pressure us into relinquishing control of the Canal. Tensions are running high. The last thing we need is an incident to spiral out of control.'

'We don't want to cause trouble,' Arno insists.

'A Soviet spy trawler just came through. The Ruskies are smuggling in weapons to stir up trouble.'

His walkie-talkie crackles into life. 'Just found a dead body in the water. Must have bled out.'

My eyes flash on Jerry, who sits hollow-eyed.

'Do you want me to call that into HQ?'

The officer goes up on deck while we sit in silence below, with nobody looking at each other. Three minutes later, he pokes his head through the hatch. 'Here's the deal,' his eyes locking on each of us in turn. 'My orders are to escort you out of Panamanian waters as quickly as possible. This entire incident never happened. Clear?'

Jerry salutes, and the officer returns the gesture. 'Let this be a lesson to us all. We live in dangerous times. Have a safe journey.' Arno nods respectfully. I swear he clicks his heels.

First light sees us heading out under the escort of a US Navy PBR31 Mk II Patrol Boat. After an hour, the *Pibber* spins away in a cloud of exhaust smoke, a whoop from its klaxon, and the Zonian slogan daubed on its transom: 'We bought it, built it, it's ours!'

***

By mid-morning, the shock of what's happened sinks in, and in reaction, I feel sick. The family huddles below, singing a lullaby together in German. The melody of *Der Mond ist aufgegangen* filters up through the hatch. It is a traditional song about the moon, the sky, and the stars, and I guess it's their way of making sense of what's happened. Incongruous with the harmonies below, I'm kneeling and washing away the dried blood. The drips from my head on the cockpit sole are like splashes of red wine, but what I hadn't noticed before is a pool of blood in the scuppers. It looks like it came from a stab wound, but that's not a question I want to ask. The violence that spiraled out of control is best left unimagined.

'I've seen an officer faint at the sight of blood,' Jerry comments, watching me swab the deck.

'Not a useful trait in a soldier,' I try to make light of the situation.

'Public school pillock! He was all la-di-da and no common sense.'

Refusing to take the bait, I toss the bucket over the rail, then drag it back up on its lanyard with enough water to sluice down the mess. With the evidence washed away, we might get back to normal.

As we bid farewell to the Gulf of Panama, the engines thrumming beneath our feet, Jerry steers us into the Pacific, heading towards Isla Jicaron. I'm on the lookout so we don't get trapped in the kelp fields off the Azuero Peninsula, where the dull grey sands stretch ahead, as flat as we all feel.

Anna breaks the spell at noon coming on deck with a brew.

'Jerry, I want to say how grateful we are for what you did.' She hands him a mug of tea.

'Was doing my job, missus. It's what you took me on for,' he replies with modesty. 'Told you pirates are about.'

Hearing the exchange, Arno sticks his head out the hatch. 'You had me worried, Jerry. Wondering whose side you were on.'

'That was the point, skipper. They had no idea what they were doing, so they could have done anything. I had to lure them into a trap with you all out of the way.'

'You didn't have to be so rough. You gave me a right kicking.'

Jerry looks at me. 'I'm a professional. I don't do playacting.'

Chapter 4

Abrupt Halt

Hearing Lucie's barefoot tread pad along the deck towards me, I stop trying to scratch my itchy cut.

'Let me have a look at your wound.' Leaning forward, I feel her hands separating my matted hair. 'It needs washing with salty water. Were you hit by the gun or the machete?'

Looking at her feet between mine, It's time to fess up, as I've regretted the split-second when Lucie thought of me as a hero. The instant I took the credit for being in the action when I was only a bystander.

'It was a shelf.'

'A shelf! Did you say a shelf?'

'Yes. The awkward one by the companionway hatch. I knocked into it when the boat spun out of control.' My voice trails off as the fine golden hairs on her legs distract me.

'But I thought you...' Lucie says, but I interrupt her.

'I'm no hero; I don't want to take credit that I don't deserve.'

'Now you're being modest,' she says, putting her arm on my shoulder. 'It must have been terrible for you.'

Wanting her hand to stay there as long as possible, I let out a little sigh. Lucie ruffles my hair in sympathy.

'Ouch,' I squeal as she touches the scab by mistake.

'Sorry, Plum. I had no idea a shelf could be so painful.'

'Now you're making fun of me.'

'Come back to the cockpit. I'll clean it up.' She leads me like a wounded soldier before raking Anna's medicine chest for witch hazel.

'Oh, get this!' says Jerry, his eyes darting back at us from the helm. 'Florence Nightingale and her poor patient. Makes me want to puke.'

I may be reading this wrong, but is he jealous because Lucie's paying me attention? Better watch my back or be pushed overboard, leaving Jerry with the girls and the contraband he hasn't paid me for.

Attitudes change when Johanna appears on deck wearing bug-eyed wraparound sunglasses, asking if anyone's seen her book.

'Which one?' Jerry says, all helpful. 'You've books everywhere.'

'*Jonathan Livingston Seagull!* I was getting into it, and now I can't find it anywhere. It's driving me crazy.'

'We're free to go where we wish,' I quote. 'And to be what we are.'

'Have you taken it? It's mine. Give it back!' Johanna says, accusing me as though I've stolen it.

'No! I've read it. It's a boho bible.'

'What other goody-goody bullshit does your bird book say?' jibes Jerry, feeling left out.

'Here's a test that tells you when your mission on earth is over,' I say with a flourish.

'Oh, yeah, what's that?'

'If you're alive, it ain't.'

Jerry is at a loss for words, questioning whether what I said is stupid or smart, as Johanna departs to continue her journey.

'She fancies you,' I whisper, hoping to wind him up.

His eyes widen with excitement. 'Really? You think so.' There's a hint of hope in his voice, as though he's won the lottery.

'You're dangerous. Women dig the scent of a bad boy.'

He's giddy at the prospect of where it might lead. 'She's asked me to teach her fishing.'

'There you go. Done deal. You're in.'

'Well, she's a good catch.'

Sensing he's taken the bait; I play with his head. 'Men reckon they're the kings of the fishing hole, but once a chick's got you on the line, there ain't no wiggling off.'

'Says that in one of your books, does it?'

'No, mate. Spun it out of thin air.'

'But you're no angler.'

'No, but I know Johanna's after getting her hook into big fish, so she's probably practicing on you.'

'Ouch, low blow,' he says with a wry grin, trying to play it off as if it hasn't bothered him. But I reckon I've struck a nerve.

'Break it up, you two.' Lucie appears, having forgotten about my cut. 'I've got Papa's orders to put up sails and turn the engines off.'

Her words, a rhapsody to me. We soon have *Hoop* under full sail, and with a favourable current hurrying us along, we make nine knots.

By now, two days since setting out, we are off Jicaron Island, and if this fair wind holds, the day after tomorrow we should be hundreds of miles out into the ocean, heading northwest toward Hawaii.

***

Ocean voyages develop a rhythm. Our sea legs return by day three, and everyone's locked into the watch cycle. With *Hoop* galloping akin to a wild stallion, Lucie lets her guard down.

'One thing I love about sailing is the wave patterns. I'm calm inside when I feel the sea undulating like breathing.'

'That's how I feel.' I say, making a connection between us. 'I love all that momentum. When a wave has travelled hundreds of miles unimpeded and hits you, cause you're in the way but it doesn't care.'

'What I don't understand,' Lucie says, letting the mainsail out a tad, 'is wind. I mean, water's easy to come to grips with…'

'Just as long as it's in a mug,' I but in.

'Or, in your case, spilling it,' she quips quickly.

'You can spill wind too,' I counter, playing with the idea.

'Seriously, I can't understand how it works.'

'It's because you're an airhead.'

'It is what most men think, but I had hoped for more from you,' she says, catching me off guard. 'I thought you knew about the weather; can't you explain it?'

I lick a finger and point it in the air. 'It's coming from that direction, but I have no idea what it is and why it's coming.'

Lucie tightens up the mainsheet, and we pick up speed. 'Then it's good that I know what to do with it when it arrives.'

Hoop responds with thoroughbred class. We're galloping along today. We may be in Hawaii sooner than expected.

***

The trouble with anticipation is when the payoff doesn't come, and our balloon bursts. We've sailed 700 miles since leaving the Canal five days ago, but *Hoop*'s now dead in the water. The invisible force we rely on has vanished. Instead of a dynamic seascape, the ocean feels black and sticky. It's as if we're riding on the back of a giant sea slug galumphing nowhere.

Lucie is furious. 'The wind can't run out now,' she says, tightening the mainsheet in a forlorn attempt to beat the odds. 'We've just got started.' But it's a lost cause. With *Hoop* drifting, a sense of *déjà vu* of being becalmed in the Atlantic washes over me. The calm is unnerving when there's no end in sight. I drop the headsail to stop it flapping. We all gather for an update.

Mickie has been reading the *Pilot Book* and, similar to her father, likes giving lectures, so she tells us that at ten degrees north latitude, we're in the Doldrums, a zone that separates the trade wind belts of the South and North Pacific.

'In the olden days,' she says with relish. 'This is where they chucked animals over the side if you started running out of water.

'If we run short.' Jerry looks at me. 'I can find a volunteer.'

'Well, you'll have to catch me first,' I make a break for it down the deck. Mickie and Lucie chase after me in hot pursuit. Doubling back when Mickie heads me off at the mainmast shrouds, I bump into Lucie, and we tumble down into the fold of the sail on the foredeck.

'Oh, Plum, you're such fun. I wish I had a brother.' For a moment, we lie under the sun's intense heat, its warmth drawing our sweat away like blotting paper soaks up ink. Laughing as though we're kissing cousins caught frolicking in a haystack, we are called back to the cockpit. The change in conditions means a change of plan. Arno worries about the long journey to Hawaii and the risk of running out of diesel while we wait for the wind.

'Therefore,' he says with a finality-precluding argument, 'we are going to abandon this passage and motor north to Mexico.'

The news is a bitter disappointment as we're geared up for a long, lazy cruise. By contrast, we'll be hugging the coast all the way home.

'Will we stop anywhere?' I ask, hoping we're not going to bypass Central America.

'No!' Arno says firmly. 'Before Panama, *Hoop* has been an object of interest to people, but now I feel she's a target. The plan now is to return to civilization as fast as possible.'

'Bloody pirates,' Jerry pipes in, 'they ruin it for everyone.'

While the decision is about getting his precious cargo home, Arno reads the disappointment on my face.

'Sorry, Plum, but I can't take another risk with my family's safety. We will follow advice from the *Pilot Book* and sail one foot on the shore. You'll be invaluable on this part of the trip!'

Despite buttering me up, my interests are at the bottom of Arno's list of priorities. I can't blame him, though—our relative affluence may well provoke another incident. Anyway, I mustn't grumble, and I've nothing else to do except get to know Lucie better.

***

Hoop slices through the water, her engines humming and spewing fumes into the air. The mizzen sail flaps in the breeze as we change course. Yesterday, we sailed northwest, but *Hoop* now motors northeast towards Guatemala.

It feels like we're playing *High Seas Gamble*, my nautical game of spinning the bottle, never knowing where our destination will be. The weather, always fickle, dictates our course. We have no choice but to obey its whims.

Sailing, with all its romance and adventure, also brings harsh realities. It involves the smell of engines, frequent direction changes, and a loss of control as *Hoop* plows on regardless. I must embrace the unpredictable nature of the journey, if not the vagaries of the crew.

'Let's have a word,' Jerry suggests as we put on the cover to shield the mainsail from the sun. 'This change of plan suits us better. It means we'll be able to flog the gear in the States rather than Canada.'

'Damn sight riskier at customs.'

'You told me to trust your stash. Don't say you don't believe it!'

Ignoring him, I keep my anxiety about the proposition to myself. I'm becoming conflicted about the repercussions our plans might inflict on the lives of people I'm starting to care about.

***

Today, a contagion of cabin fever is spreading like a rash. With life confined by the port and starboard rails and the boat's length in between them, the last twenty-four hours have exemplified Jerry's description of army life as moments of sheer terror punctuated by hours of boredom. We're in the latter, in offshore quarantine where we eat, poop and sleep while life goes on outside the salty cordon that pens us in. We live in a floating tin bath of overflowing libidos, all tucked up cheek by jowl.

How Arno and Anna thought they could sail the girls around the world with a male crew on board without creating sexual tension is a mystery. It's possible that the girls are less trouble on *Hoop* than they are at home, but right now Jerry's balls are bursting.

'Keep a lookout, mate. I'm off for a five-finger shuffle.' He clutches a fistful of bog paper heading to his retreat at the stern. 'If anyone asks, I'm playing with my fishing pole. No peeking, you perv.'

'It's getting tedious, Jerry. You sound like a cracked record.'

Until now, I've sublimated sex thoughts. It's a relief as urges are usually the fairground ride to my everyday desires. I've been trying to avoid drifting into a sexual fantasy by reciting poems and snippets of songs in my head when I'm in the Coffin. Even so, whenever one of the girls passes by my bunk, their potent pheromones trigger impulses that challenge my ability to resist temptation. It makes the gay image ridiculous. But how do I break the cover story everyone has bought into? When I first came on board, I didn't fit the girls' idea of manhood. I could tell by how they responded when Arno signed me up as crew. They're used to North American jocks or athletic Germans, which I'm not. I can hardly bounce in at breakfast saying I'm straight and 'Anyone fancy a shag?'

***

To keep us occupied during this listless time, Anna, acting as chief stewardess, has us busy doing chores. I haven't had time to digest breakfast before I find myself assigned to scrubbing the deck and rubbing the rust off the stanchions. Lucie and Mickie make baggywrinkle—an anti-chafing gear for use on the rigging. They cut an old rope into six-inch bits and separate the strands, which they loop into twin lengths of whipping twine, creating fluffy pads to wrap around the shrouds where the sails rub.

'Women's work,' Jerry jeers, ignorant that men invented the stuff.

'And pointless,' Johanna pipes in. 'We've got enough for a fleet.'

Night falls, the cabin fever subsides, and we are freed from the all-encompassing horizon by a shroud of velvet.

***

This morning, a light breeze from the south blows us out of our blues, so I ready the foresail. In the cockpit, a battle of wills unfolds between Lucie and her father. In his mood of pragmatic impatience, Arno is all for cruising along with Dick and Harry doing the work. On the other hand, Lucie is romantic and doesn't want to waste the wind. They're caught in the motorsailer's dilemma, and both are stubborn. But Arno's not without heart. He turns off the engines when the wind stiffens so Lucie can put up the sails.

In awe of her ability, I help by using a pole to help the genoa catch as much wind as possible and further the cause of keeping the engines quiet. She soon has *Hoop* vibrating with efficient tension and humming harmoniously with the elements. To top it off, Lucie sets the mizzen as a self-steering gear. By connecting two lines to the emergency tiller and using the sail as a wind vane, she stays within three degrees of our course.

'It's a real pleasure to sail with you,' I say as we lounge in the sunshine, watching *Hoop* plow her furrow unaided. She grins at me with childlike pleasure. Leaning back on my elbows, I bask in her smile regardless of a sweaty arse crack from all the hard work of a relentless day's sailing.

With the coast of Guatemala now low on the horizon, we gather in the cockpit for a picnic of bread, cheese, and curried eggs. Morale is high as we leave behind the threat of pirates and the disappointment of not getting to Hawaii. Night falls: Arno steers his ship, Anna scrapes scraps into the sea, Johanna flirts with Jerry, and Mickie plays cat's cradle with Lucie.

Watching the peaceful scene, a sense of detachment begins to overcome me. Suddenly, confusion sets in, and I lose my grip on reality. My speech becomes slurred as I desperately call for help, and everything fades to black.

***

When I come to, familiar voices are whispering. I'm aware of Lucie holding my head to feed me sips of water. 'What happened?'

'You fainted,' she says. 'First, your knees went, and then you sank to the deck resembling a deflated balloon.'

'You've got sunstroke,' Anna says. 'You're to lie down and rest.'

The mist of confusion begins to clear. 'But it's my watch soon.' I protest like a puritan. 'With Johanna.'

'Don't worry, sunshine. I'll cover for you,' Jerry says generously.

My confusion passes and everything falls into place: the boat, the trip, these crazy people. Despite nausea, it's all right till I stand up and feel dizzy. Lucie helps me to the Coffin.

After struggling in, I lie cold and clammy in delirium, tossing, turning and winding the sheet around me till I'm so exhausted sleep wrestles me to oblivion. My dreams are horrific nightmares of sailing through a sea of blood with men searching for hidden treasure. Danger lurks around every corner, and there's nowhere to run.

Startled awake, I realize it's day and lie listening to the sound of *Hoop* sail on, oblivious to my nighttime terrors. Still a little shaky, I clamber out of the Coffin.

'Gawd, blimey, you remind me of a wrinkled prune,' says Jerry, sitting in the cockpit messing with a fishing line. 'If that were beauty sleep, I'd ask for your money back.'

'Where are we?' I ask, squinting in the harsh light.

Arno, points ahead. Through the haze of my headache, I can make out a featureless yet fertile coastal plain. 'Guatemala?'

'Mexico! You've been out for thirty-six hours.'

Feeling better and on light duty, I watch Jerry teaching Johanna to fish. Up to now, the ratio of fish on the table to fish in the sea is zero, but when she hooks a tiddler, she yells as though it's a whopper. Jerry helps her haul it in, and their arms quickly entwine.

Using his trusty knife, he cuts up the small fry as bait for a bigger fish hopefully, delicious mahi. He's confident these ray-finned predators are about as woody debris tangled up with floating rafts of kelp supply noonday shade for their prey.

'Mahi knows that and comes hunting,' He casts the line off the stern and lets it trail behind us.

Now wary of the sun, I go below to escape and find Arno at the chart table reading about an epic encounter he thought he'd never face. Unlike the *Kraken* or the *Flying Dutchman*, there's no denying the legend of Tehuantepec—it's got a whole gulf named after it. Lucie's understanding of wind will be tested to the limit.

Our conversation about the risks involved is drawn short by the sound of Johanna shrieking as the fishing line zips off the reel like a swarm of bees. The first mate's patience has paid off. We rush to look what's on the hook.

Jerry's stance at the back of the boat is heroic. From how he says it took the bait, jumping straight up out of the water when hooked and diving deep, he knows it's a large mahi and skillfully reels it in, tightening the line as the fish fights against him. Yet his catch turns sideways and dives when it sees the boat, forcing Jerry to play out and start over. The sheer force on the line makes the rod bend to its limit, and Johanna has to clutch onto his waist to prevent him going overboard. After a hard-fought thirty minutes, the mahi begins to tire, and Jerry shouts for the gaff.

'When I bring it alongside, hit it behind the dorsal fin and yank it up and in,' he orders. 'And don't panic.'

'Plum, you have been unwell. I shall do the honors.' Arno steps forward and shouts, 'Anna, fetch the camera!'

Removing a cork protector from the gaff's sharp tip, I hand it to the skipper. Arno, more focused on the photo than a clean strike, stabs at the fish in vain. Realizing it's a more challenging job than it appears. In danger of losing our lunch, he calls for help.

'Plum! Take over.'

Jerry maneuvers the floundering fish back to the boat. In one fluid, sweeping motion, I plant the gaff in the fish and swing it upwards and out of the water.

'Well done, Plum,' Lucie cheers.

'What about Jerry?' Johanna reward is a peck on his cheek.

Over four feet long and male by the shape of its tall blunt head, the mahi must weigh about thirty pounds—a fine catch. Arno and Jerry hold the struggling fish and Anna snaps the moment.

'Observe!' Jerry says, hunkering down. 'You'll never forget this.' He jabs the spearpoint of his dagger into the fish's brain, making a quiet crunch-pop. 'You can watch life drain away.'

We all huddle as the dazzling gold, green and iridescent blue fish fades to grey and watch in silence as a creature of beauty and strength morphs from a living organism to dead meat. Anna soon shakes us out of our sentimentality by rattling pots and pans.

After eviscerating its belly and letting Mickie chuck the guts into the sea, Jerry shows Johanna how to butcher the carcass. He guides her hand with his knife to cut behind the gill plate towards the head, then follows the backbone to the tail before cutting back deeper. There's a slight ratcheting sound as the blade knicks against the vertebrae in the spine. Johanna then picks up a fillet and lays it skin-side down on a cutting board. Lucie can't believe Johanna is getting her hands dirty. Arno jokes about domesticity not becoming her, though the smile falls off his face when Lucie whispers it might be a sign, she's getting broody.

Mickie dangles the long backbone over the side, and a gull snatches it from her hand. Jerry slides the commando blade back into its leather sheath, and Johanna proudly delivers the fish to Anna. The catch proves cathartic. We all agree it's a change of fortune.

***

The salty scent emanating from the galley makes my mouth water. Before long, we're eating slices of raw fish marinated in lemon juice, followed by grilled mahi. A subtle flavor. As fresh as fish could be.

After we finish, Jerry is given a round of applause for his catch. A doe-eyed Johanna has hooked a hero.

'You can hang your rod up for today,' Anna says. 'We have enough left for tomorrow. I will make sauerkraut and fish for supper. My new batch is ready. It was a wartime treat.'

My heart sinks. I'm an imaginative eater, but my imagination doesn't stretch that far. However, Arno's promise of two bottles of Riesling from the engine room bilge makes it sound palatable.

'I'll get 'em for you, skipper,' Jerry says, giving me a sideways look. 'No need for you to dirty your hands.'

It's then I remember the mangos I foraged from the golf course. They've been ripening on my shelf in the Coffin and have turned from green to yellow but now have a soft, mushy feel and dark spots on the skin. I slit one open, exposing juicy pale orange flesh, which oozes an alcoholic odor. While Arno looks dubious, Mickie licks her lips in anticipation. But as soon as I take the first bite, there's a terrible tingling in my mouth as though I've eaten stinging nettles or poison ivy. Rushing to the sink, I spit out fibers and gulp in fresh water.

'Tee hee ha ha!' Mickie snickers at my swelling lips. 'You look like a baboon's butt!'

Anna's quickly out of her seat and bound for the medicine chest, returning with a bottle of calamine lotion. 'You'd better apply this, Plum,' she says with a flicker of a smile.

Avoiding everyone out of embarrassment, I spend the rest of the day feeling sorry for myself. Nevertheless, by nightfall, the swelling's gone. I jettison the remaining mangos overboard. *Good riddance to bad rubbish*! I think watching them disappear in our wake.

'Told you golf's a waste of time' Jerry slaps my back in a gesture of camaraderie as he passes.

The first mate's a riddle to me. I just don't understand him! He blows hot and cold. Clearly, he's not to be trusted.

Chapter 5

Danger Zone

Closing in on the coast during the afternoon, we hear thunder rumbling in the saw-toothed mountains five miles away. At night, when I join Lucie on the dog watch, it's fireworks.

'You can see why, in past times, people thought the gods were angry,' A sudden burst of intense light casts an ethereal glow over us.

'It's still the same in Austria, called *Donner und Blitz.*'

'*Truenos y relámpagos,*' I counter in Spanish.

'*Donder en bliksem,*' she parries in Dutch.

We ran out of steam with *Tonnerre et foudre.* But then, as I catch her silhouette against the flickering white light, the mountain gods strike me with a *colpo di fulmine* as thunderbolt cracks open my heart.

'What will you do when we arrive in Canada?' she asks, unaware I've fallen for her in a way no rational argument can explain. Struggling to find the right words, I shrug my shoulders.

'You've a month to think about it.' Getting up she goes to wake up Arno for his watch. 'It's best to have some sort of a plan.'

Left alone, my mind wanders. Seeing the rugged peaks of the Sierra Madre lit by lightning, I remember Humphrey Bogart and his partner searching for treasure. After we sell our weed, Jerry and I will be as lucky as them, painting the town red and 'lighting cigars with $100 bills' while Johanna and Lucie sit on our laps dripping in diamonds. Wrapped in the warm glow of fantasy, I enjoy the last of the watch until an offshore wind delivers a dose of reality in the smell of burning, not the whiff of a good cigar, but an ardour-killing odour—smouldering garbage. What the *Pilot Book* describes as the signature scent of Central America.

Arno comes on deck. 'Take some rest. A challenge lies ahead.'

***

'Will you come and look at these?' Mickie yells after breakfast. I lean over and spot loggerhead turtles, three feet long, drifting with the current. Their curious, arched expressions appear to inquire about our intentions, a notion Mickie is only too willing to explain. In spite of a light breeze, we don't seem to be making any progress. We are sailing just to stay still.

Annoyed by our lack of forward motion, Arno orders me to drop the sails while he warms up the engines. Meanwhile, we've caught the attention of two frigate birds. They are trying to perch on the spreaders, but the swaying mast makes it impossible for their webbed feet to grip. Despite their impressive seven-foot wingspan and extended tail feathers, the birds' efforts are more irritating than distracting. Lucky for Mickie, she isn't in the rigging—given the size of the beaks, they could carry her away. Tradition is they represent good luck, though their kludged attempt at landing fuels my uncertainty about what lies ahead.

***

The constant hum of the engines reverberates through the air as we inch closer to the Gulf of Tehuantepec—a sprawling crescent bay nestled along the southeastern fringes of Mexico.

The reputation of this place precedes us. It's not merely a gulf; it's a notorious nemesis, a daunting place etched in maritime folklore. Generations of sailors have dreaded crossing these waters, haunted by the memory of relentless squalls. Tehuantepecers, those formidable mountain-gap winds, carve a path through the Chivela Pass, sweeping across the Isthmus of Tehuantepec before hurling themselves into the Pacific Ocean.

These ferocious winds, called 'T-Peckers,' can push us off course or tear away our mast with unbridled ferocity. At this moment, Arno stands at the helm, a captain confronted with a critical decision. The gulf sprawls before us as he weighs the options: the safer, more extended trip hugging the inner edge or the bolder, riskier path straight across its heart. A choice that decides whether our voyage spans two days offshore or extends to a four-day trip, tracing the coastal contours.

The best weather forecast we can find is tuning into the local fishermen's chatter on the radio; they talk of a gentle breeze wafting from the south.

Eager and spirited, Lucie exclaims, 'Let's go sailing then!'

Backing her up, I point to a dozen fluffy cotton ball clouds. 'We've nothing to worry about.'

Bamboozled, orders us to reef the mainsail and mizzen, keeping the engines running. With a two-knot current in our favour, *Hoop* should make eleven knots, allowing us to cross the gulf and be out of danger in forty-eight hours.

'We can take on any demon squall,' Lucie says excitedly. 'Plum, hoist the Yankee jib. *Hoop*'s going in.'

By the following morning, we're sixty miles into the gulf and fully committed. In the afternoon, the wind picks up and gusts up to twenty knots, creating white foam crests on the waves that whip spray across the deck. Although uncomfortable for those below, these conditions are perfect for a heavy boat. It's a thrilling sail, as you rarely have a stiff breeze blowing on your beam with a flat sea.

Making steady progress overnight, we reach the exposed section directly in the path of any gusts that might be funneling through the mountain pass. All is calm as we sail through midday with a stiff breeze, sunshine, and the water—sapphire blue.

'Did we outwit the Big Bad Wolf, Papa?' Lucie asks.

Arno taps the cabin roof, laughing as he says, 'Our house is made of steel, he can huff and puff, but he's not coming in.'

Due to the sheer joy of handling *Hoop*, we take turns at the helm while staying in the cockpit looking for bad weather. By mid-afternoon, a thin line of cumulus clouds appears to be heading towards us, often a sign of approaching weather—a forerunner of what's to follow.

Approaching the cusp of the danger zone, the wind strength

reaches gale-force. *Hoop* rips through the water as if fleeing a menace. Up ahead, a strange cloud formation appears that we try to dodge by heading inshore, but it disappears as if teasing us. Green blips appear and vanish like phantoms on the radar as Arno struggles to track the squalls building up around us. To avoid one, we head out to sea, but it grows more threatening, and then one we've avoided already re-forms to box us in. Too late to shorten sail, the huffing, puffing wolf catches us, and within seconds, a torrential downpour plunges us into a Biblical gloom. Taken by surprise and lashed by rain that strikes with the force of hail, I fight to keep control as a surge of water, propelled from the deep, catches *Hoop*'s bow and shoves us sideways.

With the compass needle swinging wildly, we are at the mercy of the elements, tossed between heaven and hell. An eerie sound whistles through the rigging, as if spectral forces are trying to steal *Hoop*'s very soul.

Then, almost as though bored, the gale-force wind leaves us stranded in a messy sea, facing miserable sailing ahead.

'Let's hope these Aztec gods have no more tricks up their sleeve,' Arno says, hastily crossing himself. 'I want to be back in a civilization I understand.'

'What the hell happened?' Jerry says, coming on deck. 'I was having a shit when the bog turned into a spin dryer.'

'A local anomaly,' I reply, regaining my composure. 'Montezuma had a last roll of the dice and lost.'

Unlike me, wondering how close we came to foundering, Arno

doesn't play the 'What if?' game. With him, it's 'What is!' He sets off to inspect for damage. With none found, he praises his German-made house of steel, then has me drop the sails while Jerry starts the engines. Arno worries that our imaginary wolf might hunt in packs.

After an anemic sunset buried behind a murky shroud of clouds, we forge ahead into darkness our path picked out by a constellation of fishing vessels shimmering in the distance. Finally, the half-closed eyelid of a slowly blinking moon guides us to safety.

***

Overnight, the wind drops and the sea goes flat. Having made it through, we motor to the fishing village of Puerto Ángel on the southern tip of the Oaxaca coast. As midday approaches, we motor into a sheltered curve of golden sand with fishing canoes pulled well back from the emerald water—a perfect spot to unwind. We slowly putter in, watched by a hunched-shouldered heron perched in quiet reflection on a rotting timber, and moor alongside a dilapidated pier built during more prosperous days. When the engines stop, the gentle kiss of a slow rolling tide mixes with distant dog barks and a braying mule. Everyone sighs with relief.

After discovering that the fuel dock is non-operational, the squat latrines are basic, and the shower is al fresco, Arno and Anna go off to find an official and record our arrival. There's a blizzard of paperwork to be stamped—according to rules no one understands— but it's the only way to obtain a tourist card and avoid arrest.

Now down from the crow's nest, where she's been looking for

hidden rocks, Mickie grabs Lucie, and free from nautical confinement, they hop, skip and jump to the beach. After they've gone, Jerry clarifies that he wants some alone time with Johanna and tells me to step out for a while.

Down the quay, wearing a hat of plaited palm fronds with a brown woven blanket thrown over his shoulder, a local fisherman is landing a catch of red snapper. He's in an old log canoe hollowed out from a tree, with tumblehome sides to help haul in nets. A collection of heavy paddles is stowed on board, proof of the strength of the wiry man who owns the vessel.

'How long does it take to catch the fish?' I ask, affecting a cowboy film gringo accent.

His voice is subdued, unlike mine. 'As long as it takes.'

I persist pretending I'm a rookie journalist from *National Geographic*. 'What else do you do here?'.

A glimmer of mirth dances within his eyes. 'I sleep, eat, drink, play guitar and screw my wife.' He pauses momentarily as I ponder his perfect life. 'What do you do, blondie?'

The question makes me feel awkward. 'I'm a boat bum.' I mumble, looking at my feet.

'It's an easy life for you then,' he says with disdain. 'My life is hard. Buy some fish and make me happy too.'

Trying to escape my self-made trap, I spot Arno and shout that fish are for sale. 'He has dollars, amigo. Sell him the best.'

'Blondie, then they will have to buy them all!' The fisherman crosses himself. 'To those who love Jesu Cristo, the sea gives up her riches, and the Yankees pay cash.'

Smarting from the encounter, I leave the shade of the palm trees and walk into the village.

***

A crumbling colonial church towers over shanty shacks on the main street surrounded by palisade fences. Behind them, agave plants protect cabbage and potato plots. Nearby, a dog lounges in the shade and chickens scratch about in the courtyard of a cantina. From its chimney, milky wisps of woodsmoke waft away on a breeze. A steel-grilled store is closed for the afternoon and, like an insect in amber, a hobbled, forlorn donkey is rooted to the spot.

Following a path leading out of the village and up a densely wooded hillside beyond, I disturb a host of fritillary butterflies; their bright orange wings brush my face. One lands on my arm to drink the salt sweat. This lush forest is hot and humid—the air is liquid.

Against a deep, verdant background, the tropical colours are intoxicating - a rich contrast with the sea's limited palette. From high in the trees, exotic birdcalls add to the heady mix.

The laughter filters through the leaves from way down the path. I creep up and look out on every cowboy's fantasy: three women are washing laundry on a riverbank a short distance away. They work with skirts tucked up and arms bare, the dappled sunlight glinting off water droplets as they throw down cotton sheets on a worn-smooth rock. With tightly drawn-back hair and splashed wet clothes, the image ignites a desire I have been trying to suppress. I barely touch myself before my seed spurts onto the rich soil. My relief is short-lived by the sight of a young boy who has been watching me. Startled he takes off to the river while I run to the sea.

***

Back at the boat, Arno confronts me with a bucket of fish. 'Jerry says he only cleans what he catches, so you'll have to deal with these and make supper.'

Taking the pail, I wave away flies. 'Thanks for nothing.'

Arno steps ashore. 'The fish were your idea in the first place.'

Never one to turn down a challenge, I put *Hoop*'s barbeque on the quay and fire up the charcoal. Then it's down to gutting and removing any scales and fins. It's a messy job, and I'm up to my elbows when Jerry and Johanna appear from the aft cabin looking as though. they've been fooling around.

'Quite the domestic goddess, isn't he?' Jerry quips.

'Looks good in a pinny,' Johanna replies, pulling down her sunglasses for a better view. 'How long to supper? I'm starving.'

'I'm not surprised, cooped up like that. But you've come too early.'

'We've got time for a beer then,' Jerry says, slapping Johanna's bum to mark his territory. She lets it pass but is not amused.

***

When the gang heads back from the bar, roasted red snapper in a green herb sauce served with rice is on the menu. Ignoring the moans about bones, the fish disappear. By the time I turn out the charcoal embers to fizzle to death in the sea, bellies are full.

Mickie's the first to spot an enterprising guy coming down the pier, pushing a trolley. Sensing an opportunity, he's here to sell us raspado, a delicious treat. Under the light of a hurricane lamp, he scrapes a large block of ice with a cheese grater, fills a paper cup, and flavors the shavings with tamarind syrup. On such a warm night, the cold, sweet, sticky raspado is the perfect dessert, and we lap them up slurp-by-slurp as the vendor leaves a few bucks richer.

Forever, the taskmaster, Arno, announces that we will be leaving shortly on the two-day voyage to Acapulco and sailing overnight as it's cooler. An abrupt end to a brief respite, but I'm spared the embarrassment of bumping into the boy again.

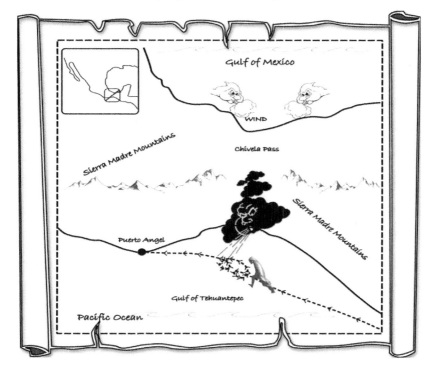

Chapter 6

Tongue Twister

Sailing northwest, we follow the *Pilot Book*'s guidance, motoring with 'one foot on the shore.' Arno keeps us so close to the beach that one leg will soon be shorter than the other. The sun is up, and our overnight respite from the heat is gone.

This morning it's hot. Feeling nauseous, I'm relieved when my watch ends. Heading below to take shelter in the saloon, I find Mickie and Anna eyeing up three cabbages bought from a market stall in the village. They sit on the cabin table like the heads of expectant pupils. With that in mind, I tell Mickie the story about my time in school when a teacher taught a history lesson to cabbages, claiming they would learn more than us pupils.

'Bet they did,' Mickie retorts. 'You're pretty stupid.'

'*Kindermünder tut Wahrheit kund*,' Anna laughs, weighing the brassicas and her child's audacity.

After much rustling in the galley lockers, Anna retrieves bowls and utensils to make sauerkraut, a staple of the German diet that earned them the nickname 'Kraut' during World War One. She serves it regularly, and although not a fan at first, I've grown to appreciate the pale fermentation. Jerry, who detests it, calls the family a 'bunch of kraut-eating Krauts.'

'By tradition, it stopped sailors getting scurvy,' Anna says as Mickie shreds cabbage and packs it into a jar to soak in brine.

'Pirates used to die from scurvy, and it wasn't a pretty sight,' I say, trying to spook the lass. 'They got ulcers, then their teeth fell out, and most revolting of all…'

'What? What?' Mickie shrieks, eager for gruesome details.

'A strange tissue spouted out of their mouths and rotted at once. Before they died, their breath smelled worse than a dead bear's bum.'

'What did they do with the bodies?'

In my best pirate voice, I make up a rhyme. 'Overboard they went, but the sharks didn't eat them, no, not a bite. You can still find them today, like dumplings bobbing at night. Rotting and putrid, it's hard to take. It'll make your eyes water and your stomach shake. The smell is so vile, so hear what I mean—one sniff will turn your pee green.'

'You're disgusting!' she squeals in delight, throwing shredded cabbage at my face. With brine dripping from my nose, I laugh as a man possessed. It's long, loud and raucous.

'Tell him to stop, Mama,' she pleads.

Anna pushes down the cabbage. 'You started it, my *Knuddelbärchen.*'

'Don't dish it if you can't take it, you little minx,' I continue theatrically.

'Stop it!' she shouts, pounding her fists on the table, 'You sound like those men the other night!' Her eyes are red edged with tears.

With a strangled cry, she bolts to her mother. Holding her close Anna quells the panic. As quickly as the volcano erupted, the terror subsidies. After a moment Mickie peers at me sheepishly and sticks out her tongue. 'Hey, cabbage head. What would your teacher say if he could see you now?'

'That I'm in a bit of a pickle.'

'Good joke, Plum,' Anna says. 'I've got a little job for you.'

Ever the maestro of mood-shifting, Anna pulls me into her homeschooling endeavors. 'You've got a delightful voice, Plum. How about teaching Mickie to read aloud with confidence?'

'Aplomb with Plum,' I declare, diving into the challenge.

Voice training was part of the Stage Management curriculum at drama school. The rationale: if a cast member fell ill, you had to be ready to step in. While acting might not be my forte, I have a fantastic voice. Yet, in the age of kitchen sink dramas and the celebration of regional accents, my Received Pronunciation takes a beating, which is why Jerry gave me one. It proves George Bernard Shaw's adage: 'An Englishman can't open his mouth without making other Englishmen hate him.'

Mickie, her tantrum, having passed as a sudden gust, is now eager to learn. We perch at the cabin table while Anna fumbles about in the galley, stowing airtight jars of sauerkraut to ferment in the dark.

'Let's start with tongue-twisters to warm your articulators.'

'What's an articulator?'

Quickly, she's tied me in knots, asking why the cartilage around the larynx is called an Adam's apple when Eve has one too.

'Back to tongue-twisters,' I insist.

'All because you can't answer my mind-twister.'

'Repeat after me! I wish to wash my Irish wristwatch.'

'Poo-bah, that's easy,' she wrinkles her nose. 'You try this one: *the tweetle beetle noodle poodle bottled paddled muddled duddled fuddled wuddled fox in socks, sir!*'

'Where did you learn that?'

'*Fox in Socks*, by Dr. Seuss.'

'Who is Dr. Seuss, and what kind of doctor?'

Mickie appears incredulous. 'Mama, Who's teaching who here?'

'Whom,' I correct her. She blows me a raspberry. We move on to practicing lip bubbles.

By the time we run out of steam, I'm exhausted. It's time for an 'Echo Lima Delta,' as Jerry calls an emergency lie-down. Sprawled on my bunk, I flick through my *I Ching* and find the passage that says, 'When the family is in order, all the social relationships of humankind will be in order.' This voyage is the first time I've ever experienced home harmony, and it feels like money in the bank. Previously, family was the sort of social currency I have always been short on.

***

My reveries are interrupted by Johanna yelling about being poisoned. Moments later, she cries out that she's going to die. I extricate myself from the Coffin, go up on deck, and find she has painted the cockpit in vomit.

Moments later, Jerry appears, also looking unusually green around the gills. Then it's Lucie's turn. She goes white before my eyes and, rushing to the rail with a cry, pukes overboard. I'm next to suffer. Prompted by a sudden churning in my guts, I race to the heads, fearing my arse is about to explode. There's no sign of Arno or Mickie, but it's safe to say they've gone down with it too.

Pretty soon, everyone but Anna is nauseous, vomiting, or suffering cramps and diarrhea. Montezuma's Revenge has hexed us thanks to the iced raspado we ate late last night. Luckily Anna is saved. She didn't eat one.

On the bright side, we haven't gotten scombroid poisoning from eating poorly cooked fish. Which, according to Anna's battered old medical manual, has worse symptoms: there's blurred vision, a swollen tongue, palpitations and dizziness. The side effects can be fatal; therefore, I'm off the hook, and no one is going to die.

Arno lies in his bunk—a fallen giant. Anna has taken command. Though we feel ghastly, Jerry and I resolutely sailor on with stalwart help from Mickie, who has gotten off lightly. Between us we shoulder the burden of standing watch and steering *Hoop* along this wild, rugged stretch of the Mexican coast. Studying the shore through the binoculars, it runs the gamut from hidden coves of turquoise water to long stretches of sand where the curling surf crashes down in clouds of spray.

We are running the engines at full tilt as we progress from Oaxaca to Guerrero. We have neither the time nor the ability in our reduced state to raise sail to catch the contrary wind. Our sole focus is making it to Acapulco.

As a reward for our efforts and to sustain us through our night watches, the variable winds, and the ongoing malady, Anna doses our black coffee with generous tots of a strong dark rum she bought in the Caribbean. I understand why the Royal Navy used to issue a daily ration. It improves morale and puts iron in bellies. I'm particularly grateful for its medicinal qualities. Badly stricken at both ends, I wear no pants and have a canvas bucket slung around my neck.

Pushed to rely more on each other, Jerry and I get on better. Possibly because the girls are confined to quarters, he doesn't feel the need to be competitive. He proves a remarkably understanding companion in my more dire moments, and I'm wryly amused by how tolerant he is of Johanna's malingering. She's let off scot-free, while Lucie, who tries to come up and steer for a bit during daylight hours, is given a hard time by him for not appearing at night.

To keep her family hydrated, the ever-resourceful Anna concocts a homemade drink of salt, soda, and sugar, administered regularly. Alongside seasickness, food poisoning is a miserable existence.

***

Now on the mend, Lucie joins me in the cockpit.

She points to a falling star streaking across the sky. 'That's a good omen.'

'What's your star sign, Lucie?'

'Go on,' comes the inevitable reply. 'Have a guess.'

Looking at the stars for inspiration I spot Regulus. 'Leo.'

'Leo? Why Leo?'

'You've something of the lioness about you.' Not being an astrologer, I guess at a possible characteristic. 'You're stubborn.'

'I'm Aquarian. And I'm not stubborn.' She proves the point.'

'Yes, you are.'

'I'm not.'

'Are.'

'Not.'

'There, told you so. We could go on like this for hours.'

She pushes me playfully.

'What am I then?'

'Aries!' Lucie blurts confidently. 'I snuck a peek at your passport.'

While we laugh, I wonder whether our constellations will align or if cosmic forces will keep us apart.

***

Outside of Arno's complaints about the fuel used to make it here, *Hoop* motors into Acapulco Bay, ready for a vacation. The city, a blend of modernist, brutalist, and vernacular styles, unfolds behind a vast semi-circular ribbon of sand, reaching out towards distant mountains. The new hotels and apartment blocks along the beach resemble smiling gritted teeth, a fitting simile for a place where US dentists escape on holiday to loosen up.

We head to an anchorage next to a luxury yacht dressed in coloured signal flags fluttering from stem to stern. It feels as though we've arrived at carnival time. I drop the hook into the green tinted water, and its chain grumbles to the bottom like the girls do when they're told the boys are off for a night out gambling.

'For a start, you're too young to be allowed in,' Arno says. 'And it serves you right for the trouble you caused the last time you went out. Also, I need to win some money so you can go shopping.'

Predictably, Johanna throws a tantrum, but before she can throw a plate, we're into the dinghy and rowing to shore.

The playground of the wealthy lives up to its reputation. A paraglider soars above us, water skiers create a lively wake, and an expensive sportfishing boat nearly collides with our dinghy. Elvis was onto something: Acapulco exudes fun.

'Did you notice that Striker 44 out there?' says Jerry. 'The first all-aluminum sportfishing boat. What wouldn't I give to buy one of those?'

'Bit out of your price range, Jerry,' Arno says.

'I might get lucky.'.

'One of us is bound to win a jackpot,' I say as we stroll into the foyer of the Fairmont Hotel. 'We've a one in three chance.'

They look at me as though I don't understand how gambling works—they're right.

Shaped to resemble an Aztec pyramid, the fifteen-story hotel features balconies with dripping plants creating a tropical paradise vibe. Herb Alpert's 'Spanish Flea' trumpet fanfare guides us to the El Cortez casino, where our three musketeers' gamble begins.

In the casino's tumult, exuberant craps players, and scantily clad hostesses surround us. Unfamiliar with Vegas-style gambling, and unsteady on my sea legs, I'm a shipwrecked sailor adrift.

'There are two ways we can play this,' Arno says. 'You can spend the evening losing your money like jolly jack tars.'

'Or?' Jerry asks, intrigued.

'Give me your small stake, and I'll turn it into something larger.'

'How?' I ask.

'I'll play two roulette tables at once.'

'Wow! Can you do that?' I ask in disbelief.

Arno laughs. 'I'm a maths brain, and while this is a game of chance, I can play the percentages. Anna only let me have fifty dollars, but if we pool our resources…

'Presuming we win,' says Jerry, suspicious of Arno's confidence.

'Oh, we'll win all right. I know when to quit.'

'When's that?' I ask, exposing my naivety again.

'When I'm ahead because I've got a cool one. You guys will lose yours and walk out broke,' Arno laughs at his joke. Jerry groans.

'A generous offer, skipper. But I'll take my chances on the slots.'

'And you Mick?' Arno cocks a skeptical eye my way.

'Sure,' I say, almost relieved, handing him two twenties and a ten-dollar bill—the last of my cash. Jerry has yet to pay me for his share of the weed, despite my asking.

Arno reads my hangdog look and hands me back the ten bucks. 'Change this into a bucket of quarters for the slots,' he says. 'Walk around until you find a punter feeding a fruit machine but not winning. Move in once when they run out of change and gamble your stake. You may go broke, but it's the best chance of a jackpot.'

The slots room is a temple to temptation; it's full of one-armed bandits—a nickname that should set alarm bells ringing. However, the sound of levers pullin' and wheels-a-spinnin' suggests that it's more about hope over expectation. Following Arno's advice, I hang around a *Wheel of Fortune* machine only to be scolded by a platinum-blond matron for bringing bad luck. I hold my ground as she's about to run out of stakes, but a bell rings and coins rattle into the hopper. Tossing me a quarter, she shuffles off laughing. I'm not as lucky after finding an abandoned *Money Honey* machine. It steals all my dough by enticing me again and again to feed the beast one more time until I've not even the dime she gave me left.

Jerry is faring better, but one glance from him scares me away, so I decide to find out how Arno is getting on. Judging from the pile of roulette chips in front of him, he's winning, but to not jinx him, I curb my excitement and keep my distance. He plays three or four chips on splits, then covers a run or surrounds numbers. Unlike the high rollers around him, the count doesn't drink but stands aloof, very much a James Bond villain. He's working to a formula and amassing an ever-growing pile of chips by decreasing the bet when he wins and increasing it after a loss. He often leaves money on winning numbers in case of a repeat. Gambling over two tables, he makes his bets according to the speed at which the croupier spins the wheel. I am watching an expert's class on speculation.

Jerry swaggers back with a bucket full of coins.

'You did okay then?' I say, jealous.

'Yup, luck of the devil. Won a hundred-dollar jackpot.'

'I lost my shirt.'

'See ya, loser,' he says with a snort. 'Got to change this shrapnel into holding folding.'

Arno wins big on number seventeen and quits. He's played the tables well and tripled my stake, even after subtracting his commission. Pleased with the night's work, we head back to the boat to celebrate our victory over a glass of schnapps.

On the way to the jetty, Jerry stops. 'Bugger, I've left my hat behind,' he says. 'Row the skipper back and then fetch me.'

'Strange guy,' says Arno as I scull to the anchorage. His opinion of his first mate wavers between rapt approval and outright bewilderment. 'He wasn't wearing a hat when we came out.'

'Maybe he bought one as a souvenir with his winnings.'

'Or he might be after a hooker,' Arno says, wise to the ways of the world. 'You might be waiting for a while.'

'I doubt he'll last that long. He's all hat and no cattle.'

'Best he finds his pleasure elsewhere,' Arno says. 'Anna worries about him and Johanna.'

'Doesn't surprise me, skipper. Must be odd having two strange men on board.'

'We don't worry about you. You're harmless, but I don't trust Jerry after the Panama incident.'

'But he saved us,' I reply, hurting from being considered harmless.

Arno regards me ruefully. 'Jerry saved himself. I have seen boys betray their own family.'

'During the war?'

'No, well before. We were so indoctrinated to the cause that nothing else mattered.' Arno peers at me through the darkness. 'Keep an eye on him for me. Inform me if he's up to no good.'

Seeing Arno back on board to a hero's welcome from Anna, I skip the schnapps and row back for Jerry. I feel I'm a servant with two masters, hoping not to fall between the stools. Indeed, 'harmless' suits my cause about the girls. And if I'm pigeonholed as not having to worry about Plum—if Arno discovers the pot in the engine room and I claim innocence, he'll believe me.

***

Waiting for my passenger—passenger and all-round prick—I gaze at local boys splitting green coconuts for American men on a late-night prowl. Their sharp panga knives deftly cut away the husk to expose the nut. The stall is a cover, a place for buttoned-up libidos to buy extra vacation delights.

With a mariachi band's romping rhythms filling the air with romance-stricken ranchera songs, unashamed men sprawl on the backseats of nearby cars, having their nuts cracked by tender-lipped señoritas. Just then, Jerry arrives, carrying a package and—in an absurd twist—wearing two straw cowboy hats on his head.

'Who's the other one for?'

'Can't have my countess getting sunstroke,' Jerry throws me a shoebox-sized bundle. 'That's gold, but not as heavy.'

'You've scored more weed.'

'The primo local produce,' he adds with a swagger.

'You mean Acapulco Gold?'

'Yup! The real deal.'

Jerry's pot is known for its taste and potency, alchemy made possible by the blazing Mexican sun and moist winds.

Rowing away from the palm-fringed al fresco bordello, I realize I'm now in deep. The simple life I yearned for is getting complicated. I'm now a drug smuggler with a killer as a partner who's fallen for the boss's eldest daughter, while I'm crazy for her sister, who only likes me because she thinks I bat for the other side. If *Mr Ching* were alive, he'd throw the book at me.

Lord knows what will happen if US Customs shakes us down. It's an eight-year minimum stretch. The closer we get to the States, the higher the stakes. What was a plan hatched in the dark now appears a tad rash in light of day.

***

Hoping for some time alone before another thousand miles at sea, I plan a day away from everyone to sort out my head.

'On the pull, are we?' Jerry says, seeing me in Speedos. I flick my towel; it cracks off his leg. He flinches. 'That's a yes then.'

'Better check the engine, grease monkey,' I say, as ever finding it hard to decide if I like or hate him. 'I'm heading off to the beach.'

Swimming to shore, I bring a waterproof bag filled with the day's essentials: money, hat, shirt, and espadrilles I bought in the Canaries. I've always looked a bit of an idiot in shades, but the glare from sunlight reflecting off of water is straining my eyes, so I score a cheap pair from one of the roving vendors selling everything from hats to handbags. Rose-tinted, they turn the crescent of bleached white sand to technicolour pink. With so many warm, inviting beach bars to choose from, I dither about which way to go. But I'm pulled up short when a familiar voice calls out my name. Lucie's waving at me. Jumping off the jetty, she runs toward me holding her hat.

'Where're you going?

'Exploring,' I say, realizing this is my chance. 'Come along with me, Lucie, let's find somewhere to have lunch together. I've got something I want to tell you.'

'Sorry, Plum,' she says, looking over her shoulder at Johanna, who is waving her back. 'We're off shopping, but I want to ask a favour.'

'Sure,' I say, knowing she didn't hear a word I said.

'I've got to find a souvenir for a friend.' She hands me a five-dollar bill. 'You'll know what a guy wants. I'm bound to get it wrong.'

'Yeah, of course, no problem. Leave it to me,' I say, but *Aaaahhh!* is what I'm thinking.

'Bye, catch you later. Love you lots,' she says, and with sand flicking up from her flip-flops, she's gone.

'And for a moment,' I say to myself, tearing off my shades to destroy the delusion, 'everything was coming up roses.'

Drinking beer under a thatch-roofed palapa, I call over every trolling vendor on the beach looking for something for Lucie's guy. But find nothing suitable.

Walking back, I stop at a souvenir shop. As much out of wickedness as desperation, I keep my promise and swim slowly back to *Hoop*, pushing a hideous wooden model of a Spanish galleon in front of me. Lucie's face is a picture when she sees it.

'Couldn't you find a smaller one?'

'You can always tow it behind as a spare tender,' Johanna quips.

'How did your shopping trip go?' I ask, changing the subject.

'They did my favourite,' Arno says breezily. 'Window shopping.'

***

Our pleas to Arno to stay on longer in Acapulco fall on deaf ears. He is adamant that we must move on.

'Consult the chart,' he says. 'We've well over three thousand miles to go. It's going to take us a month to make it home.'

'And the longer we stop, the harder it is to start again,' says Anna. 'As soon as you have your land legs back, you've got to find your sea legs again.'

'And I want to go back to school,' Mickie says to everyone's surprise. 'I miss my friends.'

After taking on fuel and water, we weigh anchor and say goodbye to Acapulco to set off for Cabo San Lucas, five days away and a quarter of the way to Vancouver. A few miles out to sea, to save Lucie from having to look at it every day, I drop the souvenir boat into the water, where it floats before capsizing and sinking to the bottom.

'Oh,' she says, 'what a shame.'

'Here, take this,' I say, handing her a package I also bought on the beach. 'This is for your boyfriend. The boat was a joke.'

Lucie blushes—a side I've not seen before—a little off-balance and delightfully coy. 'He's not really a boyfriend,' she says, pulling out a black synthetic Elvis wig-and-sunglasses combo labeled 'Fun in the Sun in Acapulco.' 'Oh, I do like you, Plum,' she says, turning it round in her hands. 'You're such a giggle.'

Mickie runs by and grabs the wig and glasses out of her hand. Lucie takes off after her. The young scamp climbs the rigging and puts on the wig.

'Lawdy, lawdy, Miss Clawdy!' She sings, gyrating her hips in imitation of the King. Drawn by the peal of Lucie's laughter, Anna comes on deck with her camera to capture another episode of the absurdity of living at close quarters. With the family antics going on, I head below for a bit of shuteye and giggle away as *Hoop* rocks and rolls me to sleep.

***

At midnight, I make a coffee and prepare for my stint at the helm. We were heading into the wind when I went to sleep, but now conditions have changed. The wind has backed and is now behind us, as I can feel we have a following sea. Oh, what a joy! I think. Tomorrow, we will be sailing again. Skipping up the companionway,

I find Johanna half asleep at the wheel.

'This is better,' I say, settling in the seat she's quickly out of.

'Don't tell Papa,' she pleads.

'Anything I need to know?'

'Just don't tell Papa.' She repeats, her words trailing away as she disappears below as though she's a rabbit running for cover.

As soon as she's gone, I realize what's happened. Instead of spending two hours heading into the wind, Johanna took the easy way and turned *Hoop* about to motor back down our course to where we came from.

No wonder she doesn't want Papa to find out! On *Gay Gander*, the skipper would have noticed we'd veered off course and been up to find out what's amiss. But we are all so exhausted the easy passage lulled Arno and the rest of us to sleep. Rather than swing *Hoop* around, I take her on a long arc back to our true course so as not to throw anyone out of bed.

Initially, my stint turns out as tedious as expected. But around the halfway point, an emergency flare goes up between us and the coast. Then another and another. I've half a mind to wake Arno but decide against it as no distress call comes over the radio. I remember Jerry's remark about crews pretending to be distressed and then stealing your boat when you come to the rescue. We've had enough piracy for one trip.

In the morning, Arno is a bit confused by our position. Rubbing his chin, he contemplates the chart.

'A strong current must be running against us,' I say, trying to save Johanna's blushes. He's not convinced. He knows his daughter well.

'We'll have two people on night watch from now on,' he says, irritated, as the squandered fuel means his roulette winnings have gone up in smoke.

***

The watch routine goes to pot anyway as *les Anglais ont débarqué*, as the French so elegantly put it. Lucie's been excused because Anna is open about menstrual taboos, so I'm on my own for the midday shift, but the matriarch feeds me coffee.

All around, the sea is as flat as an ironing board. The slick water against our hull is as smooth as Barry White. Dick and Harry relentlessly propel us forward. I'm so bored until something strange catches my eye. On both sides of the boat are dozens of creatures twisting and spinning as they stream by. 'Turtles ahoy!'

'They are Olive Ridleys,' Anna says, peering into the deep.

'Sounds like a brand of chewing gum.'

'According to this.' She holds up a reference book. 'They make annual migrations called *arribadas* to nest on the beaches along here.'

Mickie, who's joined us, leans out under the rail trying to touch one. 'Look at their funny little faces. What are they trying to tell us?'

'That that if you rush your journey, you'll miss the sights along the way,' I shout out, hoping Arno hears and we'll get back to sailing.

Pointing to an entangled pair, Mickie asks, 'What are they doing?'

'Making babies,' Anna says.

The tomboy's reply is refreshingly simple. 'Yuck!'

Turtles aren't our only visitors today. They've barely disappeared when more companions turn up to keep us company, diving under the keel and jumping from the water near the bow. With their chitter-chattering trills, squeaks, creaks, and explosions of air, dolphins are a welcome show—but I've yet to learn the lingo of the blowhole so can't answer back.

After the pod vanishes, the sea feels strangely empty. With a light to moderate north-by-northwest wind nipping us on the nose, we pass Mazatlán and turn to cross the entrance to the Sea of Cortez.

'What would you give to be on one of those, Jerry?' I ask as he comes on deck. A fleet of charter sportfish boats speeds past us after a day fighting the mighty marlin. With pennants flying and rods sticking up like lances, they resemble the US Cavalry returning to fort. Having left Acapulco five days ago, we are closing in on the southern tip of Baja California and our destination, Cabo San Lucas.

Lucie comes up for her stint on the helm, and while pretending not to look, I notice the glow on her face as the cotton-white mare's tail in the sky turns crimson, and the circle of the sun disappears beneath a darkening horizon.

'Get your head down. You're on watch in three hours.'

'Goodnight, Lucie,' I say before reluctantly dragging myself away.

'Sweet dreams, Plum.'

Chapter 7

Confident Swagger

Since the Spanish discovered Cabo San Lucas Bay, it has been a waypoint for olden-day buccaneers and modern-day pleasure seekers. When the galleon trade was founded, the bay was infested with pirates or privateers, depending on which side you were on. Several famous Cabo San Lucas Bay pirates include Sir Francis Drake and Captain Henry Morgan.

We arrive at three in the morning. Only two lights are on in town: one marks the cannery fishing pier, where we're heading, and the other is the night porter's desk lamp at the Hotel Hacienda. Letting the rest sleep below, unaware they are about to be bitten by the plague of hungry bugs already feasting on our flesh, Jerry and I moor up to the pier so quietly that we don't even wake Arno.

'Next stop, California,' I say as we finish adjusting the spring lines.

'The place to cash in and be on my way,' Jerry says, more than hinting he won't make it to Canada. 'Don't let on to the skipper, though, or I'll have your guts for garters.'

'What about Johanna?' I ask.

Jerry comes close and whispers as though something's brewing, 'She's bored shitless with all this motoring. I'll take her to Vegas.' His words sink in slowly as he builds up the picture. 'I'll have a stake by then and can become a professional gambler. We might even marry, just like Elvis.'

'Wow! That's radical,' I'm punch-drunk from a few words.

'I haven't told her yet, but she's sweet on me.'

'She's a proper catch.' I humor him. 'And you're the hooksman.'

Jerry's plan sounds ambitious, if not deluded, but I take what he says seriously. This begs the question: Where does that leave me if they go off? With them out of the way and Jerry no longer undermining me, will Lucie look at me with fresh eyes? But it's too early in the morning to worry about that and still chilly enough to make me wonder if I want to motor from here to cold Canada.

The nascent dawn reveals a harsh-looking landscape. Looming above us is an arid, cone-shaped hill cloaked in saguaro cactus, each plant standing with arms akimbo, similar to banditos in a Mexican stand-off. Also, our change of latitude is visible as tropical dew no longer drips off the shrouds. Waiting for the others to get up, we look at fish feeding on the waste spewed out by the tuna cannery, whose chimney belches out a fishy smell as it gears up for the day.

'What a stench!' complains Johanna, appearing in a man's shirt, the sleep still in her eyes. 'Mama, that better not be breakfast.'

'*Mein Liebling*, you are the rudest girl!' Anna scolds back from the galley as Arno comes on deck to survey the scene. After stretching in the morning sun, he decides we'll move to a proper mooring. Sparking up the engines, we motor a hundred yards to a newly excavated marina. The term usually conjures up images of a chandlery and clubhouse bar, but what I'm looking at doesn't fit the mold. This one is rudimentary, catering to hardcore Hemingway-type anglers looking for saltwater action and basic creature comforts. The type of rod buddies who only need a cold beer, plenty of chum from the cannery as bait, and more beer to make their day.

'Papa, how long are we here for?' Lucie asks.

'Three days. Then it's a two-week trip to San Diego.'

'This place is a dump,' Johanna complains.

'You will appreciate America all the more when we arrive,' Anna says to cheer her up. The girls haven't yet been to the States, which Canucks take to be the home of rich Uncle Sam. 'We'll be able to visit museums, art galleries…'

'Proper shopping this time,' Lucie interrupts. 'I feel a frump.'

'Johanna, you must have some things you don't need.'

'Mama!' Lucie cries, dismayed. 'Papa, tell Mama I need some new clothes—of my own!'

Peering through the porthole at the only other sailing boat at anchor, Arno pretends not to hear her. 'I must speak to our new neighbors,' he says. 'It's a *Swan*, one of the best sailing yachts money can buy, and she's heading south.' Avoiding more requests for money, he's quickly into the tender and rowing over to pick up tips about the trip's next leg. I sense that the thrill of the campaign is gone for Arno. He's now on a mission to make it home and then tell everyone how great it was.

Ever since Lucie suggested coming up with a plan, I've been in a quandary. After crossing the Atlantic, I felt clear-headed and wide open to life. But that sense of purpose has eroded, leaving me more muddled as each day passes. Maybe it's the domestic life aboard *Hoop*—as opposed to the more spiritual tone of *Gay Gander*—that's making the difference? Whatever the case, I need to regain a sense of direction rather than being swept along by events. In short, I need to know if I'm a man, mouse, or mollusk. Otherwise, what meaning does life have? We come this way but once. Best not to mess it up.

Going for a long walk is a sure-footed start to my quest if only to escape the lovey-dovey atmosphere in the cockpit. Itching to find out if those saguaro cacti are as threatening up close as they appear from the shore, I set off to the witch hat hill. I'm also curious to find out how they shape up in the dark. I plan to spend a night in the wild.

Carrying water, matches, a knife, a stout stick and a blanket, I wind up a sandy path leading away from the town. I want to untangle my thinking before consulting the *I Ching* for advice. Channeling my inner mountain ram, a rocky climb is no problem, but my sea legs let me down. I stumble, graze my knee and disturb a covey of quail.

The hill is more significant than it looked from below, and what I hoped would be an easy climb is steep to the apex, and I'm glad of my staff. Up top, it flattens into a scrubby rock plateau that might be the remnant of an extinct volcano. Apart from a goat trying to get to a branch it can't reach, I'm alone. Squeezing my eyelids shut, I turn into the wind and proclaim my mantra. 'May I find the light to illuminate the eternal now,' I chant. As I open my eyes to let the world back in, I see a vast desert extending to a horizon so distant there is enough space to encompass everything. Squinting, for a better view, there's either a mountain reflected in a lake or an optical illusion in the shimmering haze. Up here, there's no shortage of contradictions. It's a harsh landscape, one oblivious to human concerns.

***

Sitting down to a goatherd's view of the world, I consider my threefold dilemma involving Arno, Jerry and Lucie. Firstly, is my loyalty to the count misplaced? Will he abandon me at the end of the trip? Secondly, have I joined in an unholy alliance with Jerry? And lastly, Lucie. If she knew I was in love, would she care?

Unpacking my *I Ching* from its leather case and separating its fifty bamboo sticks to consult the text. I place one twig aside as a symbol for the *Tao* or that which cannot be described. With the remaining stalks, I use them to seek guidance to resolve my dilemma.

Then, it's down to reading the book text referenced by the divination. The insightful *Mr. Ching* advises that when you uproot a negative impulse, it will inevitably resurface, much like a persistent weed. Therefore, one must remain vigilant to avoid backsliding into old habits. He also suggests that you avoid compromising on corruption and make choices that lead away from evil. *Mr Ching* asserts that a restless and headstrong person will suffer misfortune. Nothing, he says, could be more specific. In a final and, for me, crucial aside, he says, 'Beware of the marrying maiden.'

What I enjoy about the *I Ching* is that it doesn't moralize but gives straightforward advice about behaving in the face of whatever's coming next. I don't always take it, but when things go wrong, I can finger the fool to blame. But that's the advantage of being born on April first; it's not a silver spoon you're gifted with but a get-out clause. Packing my trusty advisor into its leather pouch, I feel like a ventriloquist putting away the dummy. The disembodied voice dies away, and I'm on my own again. Even so, the experience is reminiscent of going to church; you only need to walk outside to lose all good intentions after hearing a sermon giving spiritual guidance. The only way out for me is to jump ship here, because our next port of call is in the land of opportunity: the great US of A.

Sensing it's too soon to leave this place and I've unfinished business here trying to resolve my conundrum, I mooch about hacking at the mountain scrub with my stick. Then, surprise, surprise, growing in the shade of a mesquite bush, I stumble upon several small grey-green cacti smiling at me with button-shaped grins. Peyote is nature's free trip, and the Mescaline Spirit has invited me to fly.

Carlos Castañeda's *The Teachings of Don Juan*, about a Yaqui shaman and meeting 'Mescalito' face-to-face, was high on the hippy syllabus, and I had read it avidly. Hence, I'm comfortable asking Mother Earth for permission to harvest and eat her peyote. Imagining a satisfactory reply, I cut three heads with my knife. After removing the outer skin, I pop them in my mouth, chew the flesh, endure the disgusting taste, and swallow.

Taking peyote is the opposite of drinking alcohol, as you have the hangover first. I at once feel nauseous; then, as the convulsions start, I begin to regret this experiment. The discomfort lasts for about an hour. Then, miraculously, the pain in my gut subsides, and the sky morphs into a swirling kaleidoscope of colours. Compelled to run, I sprint off on a dangerous downhill path. On reaching a ledge high above the earth, my arms start to windmill to stop me from falling. Inviting as it looks to hurl myself into the abyss, I fall back on my arse in a jumble of elbows and knees. My book and stick tumble down the hill alongside me and land close by when I finally come to a stop. In this altered state, they reappear as if they are long-lost friends, so I present myself anew to the world by brushing us all off.

Life's little miracles, often overlooked and unappreciated, now command the spotlight. They share the stage with iridescent lizards, their heads cocked at curious angles—one eye keenly searching for sustenance while the other vigilantly scans for lurking predators. They skitter away when a large male Chihuahuan raven lands on the path and struts about with a confident swagger. Staring at me, clearly curious about my presence in his world, he croaks his hoarse, harsh cry. Mimicking his raucous tone, I return the compliment, and we begin conversing. Our encounter is a rare connection. The spirit of a Yaqui shaman calls to me through this curious creature.

'A path is only a path, but does your path have a heart or not?' he asks, hopping close. 'One makes for a good journey; the other will make you curse your life.' As the bird leans forward, cawing, with his sharp beak, there is more: 'The child in you still wants to have; the adult wants to be. You can't turn back, so choose your path wisely.'

After a blink of its beady eye, the raven takes off on the wind, borne away to the valley below. Compelled by its guiding words, I set off, my heart racing and my feet pounding towards destiny's end.

At nightfall, under the overhang of a cave mouth, I light a fire and gaze into the tell-tale stories of the flames. When I wake up, curled tightly within the warm embrace of my blanket, dawn has come and gone. It's evening when a fisherman rows me back to *Hoop*.

***

Back on board, a party is going on in the saloon; the captain of the *Swan* has come aboard for a meal. Hospitality between boats in the harbour is a well-established tradition; it is how information is shared and bonds of friendship forged. It's also an excuse to lighten the boat's liquid payload by getting drunk at anchor—which is how I met the Camaris family in the Canary Islands to begin with. With all the seats around the table taken, I perch on the companionway steps. As every shaman in the land of tequila knows, agave and peyote don't see eye-to-eye.

Spurred on by Johanna, who's flirting with the handsome devil, the visiting captain tells of his life as a delivery skipper. He's the hero type, inspiring, able to hold his rum, and no doubt calm under pressure. But with many such men, the fellow is full of himself and even fuller of exaggerated tales of derring-do. Arno's forbidden any mention of the Panama incident, but I can tell Jerry is itching to tell, if only to put the show-off in his place. But while he's pissed off at all the grandstanding, I sense something has happened between him and Johanna. Their body language implies a change in dynamic, as she is sitting closer to the captain than her first mate. Before things come to a head, Anna intervenes.

'Enough of all this talking. It's time to eat,' Anna says, serving bowls of split pea soup. Tearing up her homemade bread, everyone tucks into the meal. Outside the temperature is dropping until it's as chilly as the mood between the erstwhile love birds. The saloon falls silent save for the clink and scrape of spoons. Then Arno has the skipper sing for his supper by giving up information about our next leg north.

'We call it the Baja Bash,' the captain says, wiping his bowl with bread. 'The journey up the coast is notorious. You'll have a short, hard chop and wind on the nose from here to San Diego.'

'We'll be motor sailing all the way,' Arno says.

'You'll need to refuel somewhere. I suggest Turtle Bay. But be sure to filter the diesel through a chamois cloth. You can find all sorts of stuff in it—even horsehair!'

'This boat can make it in one go.' Arno states proudly.

After that remark, the world crashes down around my ears. It will mean motoring to windward for two weeks without a break. The sailor inside me cries in anguish, 'Jump ship, stay here and trip out!' Too disheartened to listen to more, I creep out on deck and hear bottles clinking behind me to boisterous cries of 'Prost!'

I'm mooning away on deck, gazing upon the sea in a mood of defeat, when Lucie appears.

'Might as well stow the foresails and have done with it,' I say, unable to keep my disappointment to myself. 'It will be dull if we're only motoring from now on.'

'Oh, don't be like that, Plum,' Lucie says. 'He's exaggerating.'

'Doubt it,' I say. 'I take your father at his word.' Then I ask her the burning question. 'What happened between Johanna and Jerry?

Lucie's eyes dart furtively from side to side. 'I shouldn't tell you this, but...promise to keep a secret?'

I nod.

'Promise you won't tell?'

Nodding again, my eyes widen in expectation.

She comes closer and whispers. 'They got into a clinch last night. I mean, they've made out before, but nothing serious.'

'Well, what happened?' I say, fit to burst.

'He came on strong, a bit aroused, and she felt something. Um, like a penis—only smaller.'

'Then what?' I'm loving what I'm hearing.

'Johanna burst out laughing and ran out of his cabin.'

Lucie's hair is brushing my face, and we're trying not to laugh. I now understand why Jerry always plays with his rod or sharpens his knife—to compensate for his inadequacy.

***

Last night's carousing went on a bit too long. With Jerry and Arno side-lined by hangovers, I make the pre-voyage checks. Strange things happen on boats—fittings pop out, items fall overboard, and lines snap. There's no telling how a boisterous sea might change your day.

I'm working through the checklist when a US-registered schooner, *Maverick*, comes in to pick up a mooring. The newcomer is flying a pair of girl's knickers where the Mexican courtesy flag should be— the sort of arrogance that causes problems.

The crew resembles a gang of frat boys and cheerleaders having a good time. The sound of 'Rhinestone Cowboy' blaring over their sound system is a wake-up call to our girls.

'That's the boat we should be on,' Johanna says to Lucie. 'Not stuck here with a pair of losers.'

'Awww, having a bad day, are we?' I retort, well accustomed to her barbs. Yet, her inclusion of Jerry in the jab confirms their bust-up.

'Well, what use are you to anyone except for tidying up?'

I bite my tongue as Lucie leaps to my defense. 'Don't be so cruel. Plum's one of the nicest men we've ever had on this boat.'

'Yeah, nice! About sums him up.'

During lunch, a still fragile Arno explains the new watch schedule when a knock on the hull and the request of 'Permission to come aboard?' brings him up short. The skipper of *Maverick* has come to say hello. Brad is tall, blond and so cocksure of himself it's painful for a Brit to watch. I'm jealous. He's my age and gets to sail his parent's yacht around the Sea of Cortez with his rich pals—all expenses paid!

'Man, you've no idea how hard it is to navigate using only a road map,' he says, looking at Arno's navigation station. 'We must wait till night to see the headlights to work out where we are.'

'That is extremely reckless,' Arno says. Clearly, he does not take to this spoilt brat. 'You must never sail without charts, a pilot book and good local knowledge,' he continues, getting on his high horse as a prelude to a stiff lecture on seamanship.

'Don't worry, old-timer, only kidding.' Brad pisses himself laughing. 'We've got it all on board, charts, radios, you name it. Except for emergency flares! We let them all off last night to celebrate my birthday.'

'How irresponsible of you!' Arno replies responsibly.

'I came over to invite your kids to a party tonight.'

'No!' Arno retorts in the tone he reserves for port officials.

'Papa, why can't we go?' pleads Lucie.

'Because I forbid it!' blurts Arno, asserting his authority.

'Papa!' Johanna stamps her foot in exasperation.

'You do as your father says, young women,' says Anna, coming in as support. 'Now let that be the end of it.'

***

While we are comfortably cut off from the ocean in the harbour, Arno regularly taps the barometer to figure out the weather up the coast. Sitting in the cockpit with Lucie, Jerry and me, basking in the afternoon sunshine, he shows us the map. With Cabo San Lucas in the lee of the Baja Peninsula, once we round Cabo Falso, four miles to the west, we meet cooler temperatures, strong winds, steep waves and general discomfort even in the calmest weather.

Although Arno presents us with the choice of sailing to San Diego in two tacks, one long starboard board of almost a thousand miles out to sea and another long port board back to the coast, he's affirming his decision that we should motor the 800-mile up the coast. To lessen the impact, he divides it into four chunks, with the first one being the hardest.

The idea of a week of cold discomfort ahead, with everything soaking wet, makes being confined to barracks tonight unbearable. The schooner party is having a blast, with music, laughter and the smell of weed wafting over the water.

After a somber meal, we sit in the cabin playing cards, hoping it won't be too noisy to sleep. Thankfully, in the wee small hours, the music stops, only to have salt rubbed in the wound as sounds of sexual delights filter in through the porthole.

***

Bright-eyed and bushy-tailed this morning, I'm glad I didn't make the party as a misty mantle mopes over *Maverick* like a hangover. Four cans of beer and a bottle are abandoned on the cabin roof. A polka-dot bikini top hangs off the shrouds. Nobody moves on deck.

Possibly out of guilt at keeping the girls on such a short rein, Arno promises us lunch ashore. By late morning, the countesses are up, hungry and off up the hill to eat.

'Jerry, are you sure you don't want to come?'

'Not with Johanna. Bloody prick-tease. You'll never believe it.' He's angry. 'She comes into my cabin and tells me she loves the hat I bought her and how thoughtful I am. She's all over me like a rash, but she goes frigid when I take the big boy out to play. She claims she's a virgin, waiting for the right man, and runs away, leaving me to knock-one-out in frustration.'

'And you were getting on so well,' I say, amused at hearing Jerry's side of the story. 'All those plans you had together.'

Leaving Jerry all angsty, I rush to catch up with the family, wondering if I'll ever hear the third side of the story, i.e., the truth.

The Palmilla Hotel is built into the side of a sheer cliff, with an airstrip out back—a hideaway for a James Bond villain. The interior is classy and discreet, and Anna's convinced she saw Jack Nicholson dive into the pool. A fan of his films, she describes him as strangely vulnerable and wholly original, which makes Arno jealous.

'But wife, why do you need Jack Nicholson? You have me!' he says as we're shown our table in a cool, airy room facing out to sea.

'I'd swap you for Jack any day,' Anna says in a rare display of hurtful humor, unlike anything I've heard her say.

'What was that dear?' Arno asks, eyeing the waitress's bottom.

'Anna said what a beautiful place this is,' I interject.

'Certainly, if you admire modernism.' Arno glances around the room. 'All this glass and marble. A little stark for my taste.'

Sitting down next to Lucie, my bare knee brushes hers, and any thought of decor goes out the window as the frisson sends me giddy.

She touches my arm 'What do you fancy, Plum?'

Unable to focus on the menu, I'm as awkward as a teenager on a first date. 'Um, ah,' I stumble after a lengthy pause. 'Could you order for me, Lucie?'

'Sure!' She chooses a mixture of Mexican dishes and adds as an afterthought, 'You seem like someone who likes it hot.' After that, I struggle to concentrate on what other people are saying, dazzled as I am by Lucie's proximity and the attention she shows me. Between us, we have chicken and shrimp fajitas, fried bean burritos in white tortillas, chili tamales, and side orders of rice and plantain. As we eat, I want to say stupid things, such as 'Did it hurt when you fell out of heaven?' or 'It's nice you're sitting down instead of running through my mind.' Thankfully, Lucie can't hear them and maybe even prefers the strong, silent type. Although I sense Johanna is sizing me up. It's as though she knows what's happening inside of me. Her laugh is derisory when I spill a glass of water.

'Plum, you're all fingers and thumbs today. And you need to pick your jaw up off the floor.'

***

At the end of the meal, I'm almost relieved when Arno drags me away from the table. We go out to the balcony so he can savour an enormous cigar liberated from the hotel humidor.

'You are enjoying the trip and glad you came along,' Arno asserts rather than asking, blowing out a smoke ring and gazing at the breakers sweeping against the golden dunes below us.

'It's not without its moments,' My mind races, as now's the time to let him know I might leave before Jerry does a runner. But I'm stuck, torn between an infatuation for Lucie and the hateful prospect of motoring to Canada. But I don't have the nerve. 'We will be sailing some of the way, won't we?'

Arno, ignoring me, points out to sea. 'Will you look at that!' He shouts. 'Everyone, come quick!'

At once a crowd gathers on the balcony, oohing and aahing at the sight of a pod of orcas on the hunt.

Lucie rushes up and grabs my arm. We lean over the balcony rail, straining for a closer look. Not far away, the enormous black and white apex predators appear to be corralling something by converging from different directions into the same area. One feigns a retreat before doubling back to leap out of the water and go in for the kill. Lucie and I exchange smiles, enjoying the entertainment as if we deserve it, and it's been put on especially for us. I point out a porpoise escaping the hunt, only for a surfacing orca to slam into it mid-air and bludgeon it to death with its flukes. Lucie lets go of me to turn and reach out to her father. Arno is unsentimental.

'It is the way of the world, Lucie.'

Upset, she lets go of him and walks back inside.

'Nature is a world of strife, conflict and pain,' Arno continues, surveying the scene. "Red in tooth and claw," as Tennyson put it.'

'Is that our fate forever?'

'Man is either fighting a war or preparing for one,' He snaps his fingers for the bill. 'Learn that early and avoid disappointment later.'

***

Back at the boat after lunch, Jerry leads me to the anchor windlass, saying it needs greasing. We kneel at the hawser hole where the chain disappears below deck.

'I'm going to tell you something,' he whispers. 'When I do, don't look up.' Pretending to examine the mechanism, he continues, 'While you were away, a military-green VW van parked on the harbour wall. There are feds inside watching the marina.'

'What? Cops!' I'm desperate to take a peek but follow his order. 'How do you work that out?'

'Sssshhh! It has dark windows and a radio whip antenna.'

'Do you think they're here to bust us?'

'No. They're watching the schooner. You best keep cool and don't tell anyone. Not Arno and not the girls.'

'Mum's the word.'

'And not her either,' he says, enjoying his joke. 'Just act normal.'

Throughout the day, I struggle to keep up the façade, but trying to act normal is harder than it seems.

The Coffin offers little comfort as the snooper van is opposite the porthole. In the suffocating darkness, a paranoid scenario runs through my mind: Did our Zonian weed dealer, Scott, betray us? Even though we had told him we were going to Hawaii, I can't shake the feeling that he may have tipped someone off. It may sound absurd, but you never know.

A wild idea surfaces—what if I sneak into the engine room and ditch the evidence? It's a fleeting thought, but the family's well-being hangs in the balance. It's not long before I give up on that possibility, but I feel guilty about jeopardizing the family, which was my concern in Panama.

We committed the crime out of necessity to make money, but now I wonder about Jerry. He does have psychopathic tendencies. If they bust us, will he drop me in it? How bad are Mexican jails? All through the night, my mind plays the what-if game. My only hope is that the *Zap Comix* mantra to "Trust your stash" has a crumb of truth in it.

***

At dawn, my ears pick up, and it's no longer what-if but what-the-fuck as an inflatable boat carrying paramilitary police barrels towards us. Overtaken by impending doom, my heart pounds. It feels as though it's fit to burst.

With craft closing in, I can make out a man standing at its stern, wearing a white Cuban shirt, sunglasses and holding a walkie-talkie. When the dinghy hits our hull, I accept the inevitable. Amidst the clump of combat boots and the rattling of guns against the rails, I feel the boat roll under the weight of the men jumping on board. And like an innocent awakened from slumber, I slip out of the Coffin.

Arno soon appears in the saloon bewildered, with unusually ruffled hair. The white-shirted man, clearly the boss, comes below as

Arno straightens himself. '*Pasaportes y papeles!*' the man orders.

Arno's reply is robust. 'Please, present your authority first.'

The man laughs, revealing a police shield. 'Inspector Gonzales, Mexico City Police, at your service. I am here to search your boat.'

'Please, proceed,' Arno says. 'We have nothing to hide.'

The inspector sees an ashtray, lifts it to his nose, sniffs and puts it back. Anna offers him a coffee.

'That would be most kind. We've had an early start.'

While the percolator bubbles on the galley stove, his brutish men scour lockers and drawers. Despite Jerry's blasé approach to showing them the engine room, it's nerve racking as one peers into the void, but the other grunt whistles through his teeth when the girls show up for identification. What a relief! Men are so easily distracted.

'Excuse my fellows,' says the inspector as he flicks through our passports. 'They are not from Mexico City as I am, but peasants and rough round the edges.'

Anna serves the inspector coffee with a fresh biscuit.

'Count Camaris!' He stresses the title. 'You have travelled far.'

'And we have a long way to go.'

'I won't keep you long,' the inspector says as his men return empty-handed, but orders a second search to assert his authority. This time, they overturn the galley, infuriating Anna, who tries to take the inspector's coffee away. 'These men are lazy. They need to search properly this time.'

'What a mess,' Anna says, returning a jar of sauerkraut to its place.

'I'm sorry for the trouble,' the inspector replies, enjoying the biscuit with macho pleasure at her discomfort. 'But since the Americans pay us to fight their war on drugs, I'm obliged to make sure we give value for money.'

Draining the dregs of his coffee, he thanks the count and orders his men to leave. They reboard the boat. Jerry releases the line. He betrays a flicker of a smile before reining it in. 'That was a rehearsal.'

***

The police boat heads across to *Maverick* with a sense of urgency. Pulling up alongside, all three cops jump on board, and while Brad argues with the inspector, the other two start to search. Their work is purposeful. They already know what they're after. Back on shore, a guy climbs out of the VW van with a camera to record the scene.

The police soon haul a bale of marijuana onto the deck. The inspector barks an order into his walkie-talkie, and another police tender appears alongside. The officers arrest and handcuff everyone on board, forcefully manhandling them into the tender. Brad vehemently proclaims his innocence as the hapless smuggler is taken away. Meanwhile, the inspector secures Maverick's hatch to impound the vessel before departing with his men. The green van speeds off, signaling the end of the bust. As harbour life returns to normal, I spot the count lean against the rail and let out a sigh of relief.

'Now, can you see why I wouldn't let you go to that party?' Arno declares triumphantly as the girls emerge from below, their bedhead hair hiding embarrassed faces.

'Mama! What's for breakfast?' Mickie calls out.

'*Pfannkuchen*,' Anna calls back from her re-ordered galley.

While the family digests the events below, Jerry and I eat on deck.

'Let's go fishing,' he says when we've finished our pancakes. 'I think I've caught something.' From the stern, he pulls up a fishing line tied to a chain wrapped around our bricks of weed.

'You crafty fox!' I'm amazed by his ingenuity. 'When did you do that?'

'After that party boat came in. The first rule of combat—don't be caught in the crossfire.'

'But what if they'd spotted it?'

'You're always saying trust your stash. So, I did.'

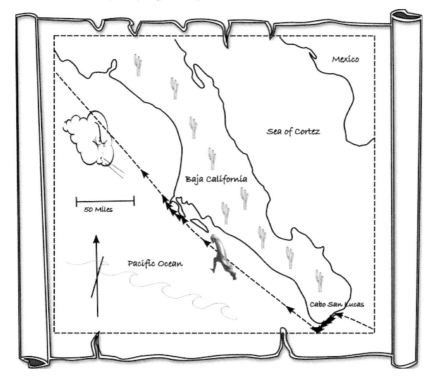

Chapter 8

Heavy Weather

'Let go of the bow line!' Arno shouts as *Hoop* slides back from her mooring. This latest episode of craziness has got under the count's skin, and we're leaving earlier than planned. We stop at the cannery pier to complete the departure clearance form and pick up a weather forecast on the way out. I'm glad we're on our way because this swashbuckling life could easily have seen me locked up in chains. There's no better feeling when luck's on your side. But will it last?

While Arno deals with bureaucracy, Anna checks our water supply. Cabo only has desalinated water, and she's cautious about mixing it with the fresh water in the tanks. I fill four spare containers, stow them below, and bring out the wet-weather gear to prepare for the soaking we expect.

'All clear ahead, Papa,' shouts Mickie from her post in the rigging, where she is watching for shoals and rocks in our path. She appears to be growing taller by the day, clearly thriving on the sea air, a varied diet and the perpetual challenges of life onboard. After rounding Cabo Falso an hour later, we make a 90-degree turn to the north— directly into the prevailing wind, which gusts around us, tossing *Hoop* halfway to heaven and giving us all a cold shower.

Having lost our sea legs and with twenty-four hours of hard sailing ahead to the closest sanctuary at Bahía Magdalena (if Arno chooses to stop) we face up to the challenge ahead.

At midday, I come up for my spell at the helm to the sound of the count whistling.

'Arno, What is it that tune. It's very emotive.'

'It's the leitmotif from Wagner's opera Das Rheingold.'

'Opera. A bit highbrow for me.'

'Wagner is an acquired taste.'

'Wasn't Hitler a fan?' I ask in a burst of self-assertion.

Arno lets out an uncharacteristically self-deprecating laugh.

'It is a Germanic myth about Alberich who is captivated by the Rhinemaidens' hoard of gold.' His lips pucker and emit a dark, foreboding tune.

'I'd like to learn that.' I say, trying to catch every note of the haunting earworm.

'Don't worry; I'll be whistling it all the way home.' He hands me the helm.

'What's our course?'

'Head northwest for two hundred and fifty miles and wake me in a couple of days when we pass Bahía Tortugas.' He laughs at his little joke and goes below.

'That's not funny,' I moan to myself. 'It means no stopping for skinny dipping with Lucie.'

With a two-knot current running against us, Arno plans to put the 'pedal to the metal' to increase our speed and make whatever progress we can against the relentless swell. Pooh-poohing the nonsense about the romance of the sea, I sing the disenchanted sailor's hornpipe:

I went to sea to see the world. But what did I see? I saw the sea.

I saw the Pacific and the Atlantic. But the Atlantic isn't romantic.

And the Pacific isn't what it's cracked up to be.

The song is tongue in cheek as I follow the barren, chamois-coloured shore along a ten-fathom depth line. This system has its challenges. In places, the soundings drop to a hundred fathoms in a perilously short distance, which means the depth-finder struggles to return a reading and show me when I am veering off course. The breaking waves knock us backward, and the constant motion turns us green. I try to bear away until the sails fill enough to help drive the bow through the waves rather than smack down on top of them. With *Hoop* heeled far over to port, at least we can tell which side to vomit over on.

***

The sea grows calmer at nightfall, and I feel better chatting with Lucie, who's now at the helm. A glance at the radar screen shows nothing ahead. However, switching between ranges, I spot a stationary group of small targets in line with our course. 'Whatever they are,' I say, 'they're not moving, and we're closing in on them.'

Taking the binoculars out on deck, I peer ahead but spot nothing except the dark water ahead.

'Might be whales sleeping on the surface,' Lucie guesses.

'Shall I wake your dad?'

The glow from the compass light shows the look on her face. It is the first time she's shot daggers at me. The flash of anger reveals a daughter transitioning from relying on her father to assuming the responsibility of keeping us alive. The message is simple: she's in charge of *Hoop* and will make her own decisions.

'He'll only fuss and ruin a quiet night. Shine the searchlight ahead.'

As soon as I sweep the beam before us, fishing canoes appear. They are floating dead in the water. But unexpectedly, they light up like a penny arcade. Lucie alters course.

'God bless radar,' she says.

'Might be illegal fishing.'

'They're more likely saving their batteries. After all, you only need light if you're afraid of the dark.'

***

After the night's lull, the weather turns nasty again in the morning. Beneath an angry sky growing more malign by the minute, we plow onward. It's more than a hundred miles to the next safe refuge. We're running a marathon, and ignoring the discomfort and exhaustion, we push on through the fatigue. Whenever we plunge from a peak into the trough of these mighty steep waves, poor *Hoop* judders with a thud. Jerry and I alternate steering the ship in half-hour shifts since the physical effort needed to keep it on track is exhausting.

'This is too dangerous,' Arno shouts from the saloon. 'Head further out to sea till the storm blows through.'

With Dick on full throttle and Harry on half, I pivot us around in a series of lurches until conditions on board ease a little. After two hours of pounding, the wind calms down, and we find our bearing again. Bone-weary, I head to my bunk. My judgment about the Coffin was right; it's wet in heavy weather.

***

No sooner has the tempest blown over than a storm in a teacup erupts in the galley—it's a domestic row over washing up, which quickly turns nasty. With Anna having done the cooking and the count excused by rank, the rest of us take turns doing the dishes while Mickie puts them away. The task is not onerous; we use seawater to wash and sweet water to rinse. The rule couldn't be more straightforward—do it straight away—except Johanna has decided it doesn't apply to her.

What brings it to a head, and why I'm furious, is that last night's dishes nearly killed me. Johanna says she's done the dishes, but she hasn't. Instead, she put the full washing-up bowl in the cockpit scuppers, in an 'out of sight, out of mind' way of doing her chores.

Like an accident waiting to happen, when I go out on deck to check an unusual rattling noise, I step straight into the soapy dishwater, slide on the plates, crash into the rail, and nearly tumble over the side. She can't understand why I'm so pissed off.

'I was going to do them later,' Johanna says, as though it's an excuse when I confront her in front of the others this morning.

'What's the good of later? You nearly killed me.'

'Don't be so dramatic,' she says dismissively. 'You fell over.'

'Almost overboard, you bitch,' I shout back in righteous indignation. 'What about the shark? I could have been torn to bits.'

'Now calm down, both of you,' Anna interrupts, her hands flat on the table in her no-nonsense manner. 'Johanna, apologize.'

'No! You heard what he called me. He should be apologizing!'

'Oh, so it's my fault now, is it?' I'm scarcely able to contain myself.

'Can't I get any peace here?' Arno's angry exclamation from the chart table breaks the tense silence. 'I'm busy trying to plot our course. Do you want us to get home or not?'

'I want to get off now,' Johanna says, her voice trembling with the effort to hold back tears. 'I want to go home.'

'That's right, turn on the waterworks,' I snap, frustration evident in my tone at her childish behaviour.

'I hate you,' Johanna retorts, her words laced with venom, aware that I've seen through her façade.

'Is that why you tried to kill me? Premeditated murder, was it?' I counter sharply, the accusation hanging heavy in the air. 'You could hang for that.'

'We don't have the death penalty in Canada,' Johanna counters calmly, her logical reasoning surfacing beneath the storm of emotion.

'No, but in the US they fry anybody.'

Arno steps in, putting his foot down. 'Enough of this bickering. In two days, we'll be in San Diego. I'll leave you both there if you don't stop.'

'Why am I getting the blame? All she needs to do is her chores.'

'Chores for bores.' Johanna smiles getting in the last word.

***

Out on deck with Arno humming away at the helm, it's time to enjoy the stars. With no moon tonight I can make out the Pole Star leading us home. Due to its position on the Earth's axis, Polaris remains fixed in the sky, and its altitude directly corresponds to our latitude, which lies between the Sahara to the south and Taiwan to the north.

Arno's perspective is more poetic, and he waxes lyrical:

'*Such' ihn überm Sternenzelt!*

Über Sternen muß er wohnen.'

'What does that mean?' I ask, feeling like a *dummkopf*, one of the few German words I've learned from him.

'Seek him above the starry canopy! Above stars must He dwell,' Arno says, slipping between tongues.

'Where's it from?' I ask, again showing my ignorance.

'It is the poem *An die Freude*, by Friedrich Schiller, or the *Ode to Joy*, as you English call it.' Arno explains it's about finding proof of God in the wheels of the universal time machine.

'You'll never observe his vision as clearly as we do tonight. As a child back home in the great mountains, I saw the stars, and their coldness frightened me. Now, they are old friends.'

'Do you believe in God?' I ask.

'Most people believe in things that are implausible, impossible or plain stupid,' Arno says, as though it's an equation. 'They accept them because other people tell them they should. I saw a world torn apart by beliefs forced on me, so now I have no fixed opinions.' Adding after a pause. 'To paraphrase Voltaire, Doubt is uncomfortable, but certainty is ridiculous.'

***

We are now three hundred miles from San Diego. To give us a break and to prepare for the final push, Arno navigates into a tiny cove on Cedros Island. Here, we drop anchor mid-morning and turn the engines off. Desolate and remote, it's paradise.

All about the boat, coloured triggerfish skitter about, their sickle-shaped tail fins dancing in the shallow, dappled water. By comparison, vegetation on shore is minimal, with a few blades of grass peeking out from the wind-scoured rocks. A flock of sandpipers feeds along the water's edge, and a noisy family of seals barks at our approach. It hardly seems worth going ashore. It's an opinion not shared by Mickie, who leaps from the stern into the water with arms and legs outspread as though she might fly. She's then followed by Lucie wearing a bikini and Johanna in a wet T-shirt, revealing nipples pert enough to make Modesty Blaise blush.

'Aren't you coming in, Plum?' Lucie shouts.

'Someone's got to stay on board,' I call back, seeing Arno with snorkel and flippers, flop into the water.

'You go, Plum,' Anna says, handing me a net bag and shooing me away. 'Find what you can forage from the rocks.'

Diving in, I aim for where Lucie's treading water, grab her ankles and pull her down. Letting go, we both bob to the surface. She enjoys the game, puts her hands on my head, and ducks me under. My face brushes her naked belly, and then her legs scissor my neck and squeeze me into her crotch. My hands reach up to clench her buttocks before sliding down the back of her legs to separate them and work myself free. Can I risk a kiss? But the moment is gone as, through blurry eyes, I watch Arno swim by, speargun in hand. Still grappling, Lucie and I struggle ashore, disturbing a small ray that darts away. We scramble onto the beach and fighting the surge of the tide we wrestle in the waves—the frolic ends when Jerry kicks sand in my face.

'Sorry, mate, couldn't resist. Always have been a spoilsport.'

'Couldn't keep up with her then?' I point to Johanna down the beach by way of a comeback.

He looks forlorn. 'The one that got away.'

'Don't worry, Jerry,' Lucie says, bending to shake the sand from her hair. 'She'll only break your heart in the end. Best get it over with.'

'Plenty more fish in the sea,' I say, throwing him the net sack I've tucked into my Speedos. 'Let's find what we can forage for lunch.'

'And I thought you were pleased to see me.'

The outgoing tide reveals a wealth of clams, which we scoop up by hand from shallow pools. Jerry returns to the boat with a sack full to hang in deeper water and filter out the sand. Meanwhile, reverting to childlike curiosity, Lucie and I go tide-pooling, turning over rocks to find sea stars, anemones, limpets, crabs, and a sea cucumber, which is best left alone. An idyllic hour of innocent pleasure passes before Johanna and Mickie return from beachcombing. We tear ourselves away from this enchanting shoreline and swim back to the boat.

In spite of Johanna's T-shirt drying out on her, Jerry is off in a huff, bravely trying to fish from the stern. I scoot down the companionway to find a change of clothes, and Lucie slips out of her bikini and into a loose muslin shift. Seeing her sun-kissed, radiant body is utterly distracting, but Anna hands me a bowl of steamed clams, garlic, and pasta, bringing me back to reality as I carry it to the cockpit for lunch.

We all cheer when Arno returns having speared a moray eel. He gives it to me to skin and clean, which I'm happy to do, but not before taking a siesta under an awning rigged over the boom.

***

Later in the afternoon, I move to the foredeck to deal with the repulsive looking but delicious eel. I'm struggling to tear off the mucus-covered skin when Jerry joins me. We talk about fishing until Mickie, up in the rigging, points out a dark shadow looming in the water six feet away. A triangular dorsal fin cuts through the surface, and an atavistic dread overtakes me. It's a shark—the first I've seen.

'They always have that effect on people,' Jerry says. 'We must be hard-wired to be scared of apex predators.'

'What do you do if you're swimming, and one comes by?' I ask, thinking of us all swimming in there earlier.

'The trouble with sharks is that they're curious. They check you out by brushing past, but since their skin is as rough as sandpaper, you end up bleeding. Once blood's in the water, it's game over.'

'What about punching them on the nose?'

'You couldn't punch your way out of a wet paper bag,' he says. 'Sharks are out of your league.'

'You could be right.' I lean over the pulpit rail to observe the gathered beasts. Unexpectedly, Jerry lunges at me from behind, grabbing my arms and pretending to throw me overboard. I wrestle myself free, turn and land a punch on his unsuspecting chin. 'Ouch!' He staggers back rubbing his jaw. 'Might have to revise my opinion.'

'Stop mucking about and throw them the guts,' Mickie shouts from the rigging. 'I want a proper fight.'

Within seconds of tossing in the entrails and head, with its razor-sharp teeth, a frenzy of badass sharks scrap among themselves.

Later, as the last rays of light shoot across the western sky and the fireball sun slips below the horizon, we clear the decks for action. When Arno starts the engines, everyone knows it's time to leave our playground paradise. Taking the helm, I spot Lucie sitting on the bowsprit facing out to sea. I yearn to join her, but I'm tied to my post. She's only forty feet away, yet it could be miles. I imagine her saying goodbye to the barefoot life she's lived for the last year. Our next stop is the USA. A different way of living.

***

We spend the next two days motoring three hundred miles along northern Mexico's coastline under a relentless sun or cold, indifferent stars. This part of the journey feels as though we're driving on a two-lane blacktop through a desert, with mile after mile of nothing happening. But as we make it closer to the US border, there are signs ashore of rapid development. Through the binoculars, I can spot newly constructed motels, shopping malls, and beach resorts stretching from here to Ensenada.

Mickie spots fast-food burger wrappers among the flotsam drifting south in the water. We're now within spitting distance of the Land of Plenty, so she starts nagging Arno about having a birthday meal with Ronald McDonald when we arrive. I am less enthusiastic. I feel anxious and troubled by my failure to get close to Lucie, who now seems distant since those magic moments we shared on Cedros Island. Is it because we're not sailing that we now have no mutual interest? Or did our fun and frolicking cross a boundary?

Once we have time alone, I'll tell her how I feel. But how do you go about telling someone you love them? What does the word even mean, and is it right to love them without their permission? Then I kick myself for brooding. It's a bad habit I'm getting into, particularly tonight. *Mr. Morbid* turns up as an uninvited guest and hangs around until the party's over.

***

We are sixty miles from the border this morning. Our proximity to the US has galvanized Arno, who appears on deck wearing a new yachting jacket and calls a general meeting. The incident in Cabo San

Lucas has made an impression on him, as he's anxious we don't come across as 'rum runners'. He orders us to dress smartly, behave courteously and remember that a smile goes a long way.

'Who wants eggs for breakfast?' Anna asks at the end of his pep talk. 'I've got lots to be rid of, as it's illegal to take them into America. We don't want to break any rules.'

Uncharacteristically, I shake my head. I'm sick to my stomach with worry. What was an abstract concept weeks ago in Panama turned into a close shave in Cabo and is now morphing into an anxiety attack as we steam toward the customs dock. Going to the heads, I puke. After giving myself a talking-to, deep breathing saves the day.

With everyone prepped, we pass the barren Coronado Islands, and Arno plots our position relative to the lighthouse. Standing on the deck, clean-shaven and ready for muster, I raise the yellow Q flag in anticipation of clearing customs. As we pass the red-and-black buoys marking San Diego Bay's entrance channel, Arno lets both engines rip, and we race down Imperial Beach, the US courtesy flag snapping in the breeze. On our way in, we pass two nuclear submarines lying low in the water next to a Navy complex of fuel tanks and double-jib cranes. While I take it all in, four Huey helicopters swoop over us, and the staccato thunder from their rotor blades reminds me that, regardless of losing in Vietnam, this is the primary base from which the United States projects its power across the Pacific.

We arrive at the Shelter Island Port Authority Dock, greeted by a line of fast-looking police boats. Standing on deck, mooring line in hand, I feel my guts turn to mush at what might happen next.

Sensing my trepidation, Jerry remarks, 'If you don't start trusting the stash now, I'll shove the anchor up your arse.'

Two Immigration and Customs Enforcement officers come on board. Their first concern is illegal food and plants.

'Someone brought in one piece of contaminated fruit a while back. The pest outbreak cost California twenty million dollars.'

The immigration officer, who's never processed an actual count before, defers to Arno, addressing him as 'your excellency' and is duly impressed by his extensive logbook.

'What a pleasure to have a real adventurer stopping by,' he says. 'Ain't many folks do what you have done. Look around this marina.' He gestures with a broad sweep of his arm in the general direction of the harbour. 'We've thousands of pleasure craft moored up here. Where do they all go? What do they all do?' He's not a man to wait for an answer. 'Most of them do nothing. Their owners come down at the weekend to sit in the sun and drink beer. You've been halfway around the world and are heading up the coast the hard way. I admire you and your brave boat and crew. I bet she's got powerful engines.'

'Do you want to see them?' Jerry offers.

'Sure, be great! Nothing beats the smell of well-oiled horsepower.'

'Follow me,' Jerry says, leading him to the engine room hatch. The customs officer notices how cramped access is. Being a large guy, he flashes his torchlight around. 'Awesome,' he says as the beam picks out Dick and Harry's gleaming copper and brass pipe work. 'They've got you this far. They'll get you home.'

'Oh, yes,' says Jerry. 'They're well looked after.'

'I'd better go back and finish my job.'

The Camaris family, being Canadians, are processed without a hitch, while my multiple-entry US visa proves its worth. Jerry is not so lucky. With no visa, he must stay on board under the Innocent Passage regulation until we get to San Francisco. After their brief examination of the boat, more out of curiosity than scrutiny, I lower the Q flag. We are now officially in the US of A.

Once refueled and watered, we move to a *Silver Gate Yacht Club* guest mooring as Arno's *Seven Seas Cruising Association* membership entitles us to reciprocal privileges. No sooner are we moored up than it's a rush to the showers. The girls head off, purring at the thought of hot water and shampoo, while Arno and Anna head off to make themselves known at the clubhouse. They leave Jerry and me to wash down the brightwork with fresh water. With the hose pipe on and brushes in hand, we have a pow-wow.

'You need to find a buyer for the weed, pronto,' Jerry says.

'Isn't that too risky? We could be ripped off and lose the lot. Let's wait until San Francisco. I have a friend there I can trust.'

'I can't wait that long.' He scrubs a reluctant salt stain. 'I've never been to the States before. You have. Find a pothead and work it out.'

'You're asking a lot, Jerry.'

He gives me a smile that belies the anger in his eyes. 'Oi sunshine! What the fuck do you think happened back in Panama?' He pulls out his commando knife, weighing it in his hand. 'Without this baby, you'd be dead!' Jerry lets the words sink in. 'You wondered where all the blood came from? Well, I stuck that pock-faced little fucker in the groin. You should have seen his face when I pushed him over the side. He didn't want his mummy, like most dying pricks. He wanted his cock back.'

My blood runs cold as my brain processes this grim image.

'Now I've got your attention,' he says, glowering. 'Let me make it plain. I saved your life. Get out and find a fucking dealer. Otherwise, I'll add your balls to my collection. Is that clear?'

Recovering from this onslaught, my brain fog lifts. Regardless of his bluster, Jerry's stuck without my help. 'OK, partner. You don't need to threaten me. I'll do it, but only if you say pretty please!'

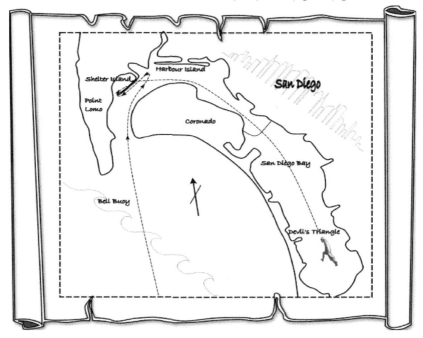

Chapter 9

Rusty Hulks

Nothing focuses the mind better than an ultimatum, so I step off the boat to escape from Jerry and formulate a plan. The nearest chandlery is always a good place to gather valuable local knowledge.

The local boatyard store is a little dusty and disordered, with stock ranging from state-of-the-art gear to kits reminiscent of what Noah might have needed for his Ark—the type of place where you might expect to find the fabled tin of tartan paint. Behind the counter stands a guy with a goatee beard and aviators.

'Whatcha lookin' for, dude?'

'You got any fog locker's in stock?'

He chuckles, recognizing the sailing joke. 'Far out! Fog lockers, man! Sorry, dude, I sold the last one this morning.'

'Oh, that's a shame,' I reply slowly, weighing each word.

'Hey! Is that an English accent, dude? You off the Canadian yacht that came in? What's your name? I'm Skuz.'

Business is slow. We engage in banter. Skuz is fascinated by my trip, and as with many Yanks I've met, he's open, helpful, and friendly. It seems we're on our way to becoming friends. Sensing I can push my luck, I raise the subject of weed.

'Where can a guy get high here?' I ask. 'I've been cooped up with a bunch of straights for too long.'

'Captain Morgan would sure dig to hear your story about the hijack. Come along with me tonight to the Devil's Triangle.'

'What's that?'

'A8! It is the only free anchorage left in the United States. The home of the brave and the sea of the free.'

'Whereabouts?'

'Under the bridge and not far away,' he points upriver. 'Home to the South San Diego Bay Guild of Pirates. That's where the action is. You up for it?'

'You bet your sweet sorry arse I am.'

'It'll blow your mind. It's full of batshit crazy dudes.'

'How do I make it back?'

'Once you have been to Hell, there ain't no comin' back,' Skuz senses my concern. 'Don't worry, dude. I'll make sure you come out alive. Those new fog lockers are coming in tomorrow, and I need to make a sale.'

'Snap to that!' Hoping this is a promising start to a deal.

After agreeing on the meeting time and place, I head back.

Jerry can't play hardball with the others back on board, so I stall before breaking the news to him.

'Goodness me, Anna! You scrub up well. Is that a skirt?'

'I have to impress the Fritzingers,' she fusses, adjusting a blue silk scarf. 'They are members here, originally from Austria, and have invited Arno and me for supper in the clubhouse.'

'Well, you look great.'

'And Johanna, Lucie and I are going to watch TV,' Mickie chips in. 'They've got a lounge with comfy chairs.'

'I'll stay here and babysit Jerry,' I say as they all clamber on deck and head for the yacht club.

'OK, Plum you've had your fun. What's happening?'

***

Irritated that he can't come along, Jerry accepts that going to the Devil's Triangle is a way forward. I pass him an empty cigarette pack I found in the trash to fill up with our gear as dealers sell dope here by the 'lid'. We'll need to sell lots more, but it's a sample I can take to test the market. While Jerry goes to the engine room, I chill my inner panic and channel my inner cool.

'Here.' He throws me the pack. 'Tell them Panama Red's in town.'

***

Clandestine in the military surplus inflatable, I hold on tight as Skuz, his cop shades reflecting the shore lights, motors us up San Diego's boot-shaped bay. Compared with the Panama Canal, this water is sour milk, as acres of urban development have taken their toll. What was once a fertile, shallow bay ringed by salt marshes and mudflats is now a toxic wasteland.

To disguise its embarrassment, a wind springs up when we pass under the Coronado Bridge. We plow through a bit of a chop, bumping from crest to crest on a roller coaster ride, the spray stinging my face like a brutal lash. When a motley collection of derelict cargo boats and barges hove into sight, Skuz revs the outboard to maximum thrust, and we speed towards the notorious A8.

Resembling a circled wagon train, the rusting hulks shelter a shamble of sailboats, catamarans and motor launches, all too renegade to find a berth in a swish marina. As we slip through the cordon of floating obstacles, a junkyard dog howls out a warning.

'He smells stranger, and stranger means danger, dude.'

In the middle of this watery outpost, festooned in coloured lightbulbs, a Mississippi-style riverboat is perched precariously on a half-sunk barge.

'That's Neptune's Palace, dude. The best party boat in the bay, owned by the Devil himself.'

After tying up, we walk down the boat's painted wooden veranda, push through saloon doors and enter the belly of the demi-monde. Inside, a mirror ball revolves from the ceiling and sends fireflies of light flickering over the faces of transients, sleazy yogis and stoned poets. "Mama Told Me Not to Come" blares from a sound system somewhere—It's my kind of place!

Loping up to a bar stool, Skuz gets his regular beer while I attract attention. 'Hi, stranger, I'm Tammy,' the barmaid says. 'What's your poison?' She has red bedhead hair, only a hint of makeup, and enough character in her face to be wickedly attractive.

'A cold one, please, Tammy,' I reply.

Amused by my accent, she rips the cap off a bottle. 'Go for the gusto, Limey, or don't go at all. That'll be a buck.'

'In that case, can I smoke a joint in here?' I ask, pushing a two-dollar bill across the bar and not expecting change.

'Dude, you're on a pirate ship,' Skuz answers. 'A thousand laws say you can't, and none apply here.'

Tammy flicks me a pack of American Dream rolling papers.

'This dude's a fucking hero,' Skuz says, doing the heavy lifting for me. 'He saved a family from getting hacked to bits by pirates.'

'Well, Mr. Hero,' Tammy says, 'I'm a girl in need of rescue myself.'

'Yup! Usually about closing time,' Skuz spins me his Zippo.

With the rolled joint between my thumb and index finger, I apply a gentle flame to the tip, slowly rotating it while blowing on the end—the first toke bursts with a flavor of grapefruit. I take the smoke deep into my lungs before exhaling; a sweet, earthy aftertaste lingers on my tongue. I pass the joint to Skuz, who sniffs the reefer like W. C. Fields does a cigar.

'Is this what I think it is, dude?' he asks, as though spring has come, and he can smell new-mown hay.

'Yup!' I say, as my mind settles serene. 'Panama Red.'

In a flash, Skuz and the joint vanish—I swear I hear the puff! Tammy smiles. 'He's Morgan's eyes and ears.' She points to a spiral staircase going aloft. 'You move fast, Limey. You'll get an invitation to the captain's table.'

'Why?' I ask as my body and mind tingle.

'Panama Red is Morgan's weed of choice. There's been a drought.'

The staircase rattles. Skuz calls me over.

Tammy leans across the bar. 'When I come off shift, turn me on.'

'Let's go, Dude!' Skuz shouts. 'Before you fall off your chair.'

With a deal to be done I tear myself away from Tammy like a sticky plaster off a leg.

***

Following Skuz upwards, I screw out of the helical hole of the staircase into the pilothouse of this mud-stuck riverboat. Captain Morgan stands tall by a panoramic window, gazing at his watery domain.

He's moustachioed with a square jaw. 'How come you swim into Neptune's Palace with the best weed in the world?'

'The devil works in mysterious ways.' I toss him the pack.

Spilling the florets onto a desk, he checks them with an expert eye.

'Skuz says you're just passin' through.'

'Yeah, heading to LA to meet my contacts,' I lie.

'Do you have any product you might care to leave in San Diego?'

'Since you're having a thin time of it, and fate has brought us together, I'm sure we can come to an arrangement.'

'Skuz tells me you've been playing heroics with pirates in Panama. I hope you won't try that here. We're a different breed of buccaneer.'

'Not unless you've a machete,' I bluster.

'Nope! Never get that close. I carry a Colt 45.'

We strike a deal including the Acapulco Gold in return for a bundle of cash tomorrow afternoon.

Leaving the Captain with enough pot for him and Skuz to get wasted, and a promise of a lift back in the morning. I head downstairs in the hope that Tammy's off shift. I'm not disappointed. The bar's empty, and the mirror ball's stopped spinning.

'Well, stranger,' she says, as I close her warm palm around the flower buds. 'Let's see if Panama Red lives up to his wild reputation.'

'What's that?' I ask, as she leads me down into the cabin deck.

'Remember that old cowboy tune.' Her voice wraps around me in a warm embrace. *Panama Red, Panama Red rides into town and takes me to bed.* As we slip behind a damask curtain into a jasmine-scented bedchamber, the fringe benefits of international crime soon become clear in this purely transactional world.

An early-morning mist rises from the water like steam off a witch's cauldron. Skuz and I quietly work our way out through the maze of ramshackle boats piled high with barrels, tarps, and other miscellaneous items that might come in handy someday. The junkyard dog is fast asleep as we head back down the bay.

We silently glide through the water for three miles. After giving Skuz the rest of the weed for the taxi ride, I agree to meet him later to go back and meet the Captain. 'Don't get hung up about Tammy. She's a one-time girl. Her old man's doing time. He owns the dog.'

***

Slipping into the Coffin before anyone else is awake, I lie exhausted, listening to halyards slapping the mast—is *Hoop*'s alter ego tut-tut-tutting me? It's not long before Lucie prods me back to reality.

'Where were you last night?' She's half curious and half angry but only half showing it. Grabbing my pillow I try to hide.

'Lost my way in the dark,' I whisper, aware of lying to her—again.

'Let's get going, children!' Anna shouts out. 'Time to move.'

'What's happening?' I ask, peering from behind the pillow.

'The Fritzingers took pity on Mama and decided she needs a break. They've invited us all to stay the weekend at their ranch in Spring Valley. We'll go horseback riding. They've got a pool. Tennis courts. Everything!'

'Well done, the Fritzingers. Sounds as though you'll have fun.'

Hearing them all leave in a chatter of excitement, I lie in my bunk, thinking about last night and how it turned out. I can still smell Tammy as I fall asleep. Next, I'm dreaming about the two of us in the Coffin, but Lucie finds us and starts shaking me. I wake up. It's Jerry wanting to hear what happened.

'How's the mission going?' He brings me coffee for the first time.

Omitting the last chapter, I give him an account of last night.

'Do you trust him?' Jerry asks, liking what he hears but refusing to be impressed by my fast work and negotiating skills.

'He's the pirate king and bound by the honor of the pirate code.'

'Bugger, the code! Does he have the money?'

'Well, you'll find out later when we go visit.'

Jerry's uncharacteristically hesitant. 'My visa starts tomorrow.'

'This is undercover ops, Jerry. I'm not going back without you.'

The thrill of the chase snaps him back in the game. 'Right! Let's put the show on the road.'

Leaving Jerry to put the gear into a holdall, I go off to find Skuz, but the chandlery is closed. He's not around. It's not good news.

'Our contact's AWOL,' I tell Jerry. 'I can't find him anywhere.'

'I thought you said he was dependable,' Jerry replies, pissed off.

'We won't make it to Neptune's Palace without him.' I feel the plan fall apart.

Jerry's not to be put off. 'You've sailed the Atlantic, for fuck's sake. Exploring a bay, no matter how big, can't be that hard.'

'The Bay's a mile wide. I don't know how we'll find it,' I fret.

'It's not how we will find it, sunshine. You can navigate. Work out a course and don't forget the fucking compass.'

***

Hoop's tender is unfit for the job, so we requisition her spare inflatable and drag the bag from the Lazaret locker. I set about it with a foot pump while Jerry checks the fuel for the outboard. Once assembled, we launch the craft using the mizzen as a crane. After a brief sea trial, we set off with emergency oars, a compass and a bag of weed. Together, we quickly assess the risks we are running.

'The only way to ensure a smooth operation is through fear and respect, so I'm going to play the hard arse,' Jerry says. 'Follow my orders and don't ask questions. If I make a threat, I'll carry it out.'

We make for the Coronado Bridge, where I set a course for the A8 anchorage and our date with Captain Morgan.

'We won't spend more than a few minutes delivering the product,'

Jerry shouts over the noise of the outboard. 'Get in, get the money and get out. No dawdling or small talk. It only makes for trouble.'

Enough said. We fall silent, keeping one ear on the Honda's reassuring running noise and one eye out for any hazards. Once the rusting hulks come into view, I steer while Jerry checks his weapons.

Though Morgan may have spotted us from his eerie atop Neptune's Palace, the junkyard dog heralds our arrival. When we burble up to the gangplank, Morgan's waiting. He holds onto the painter while I clamber out, leaving Jerry in the Zodiac.

'Where's Skuz, and who's he?'

'Your mate was late. This is my business partner.' Jerry nods and keeps the outboard running.

'Do you want to come inside and have a drink?'

'That's kind of you but we're on a tight schedule.'

'Let's take a look at the merchandise.'

'I'll show you ours if you show me yours.'

Jerry passes up a brick of weed he's opened with his knife.

Morgan unzips his windcheater and takes out a billfold of hundred-dollar bills. I spot the grip of a revolver in his waistband and eye-telegraph Jerry, who exposes the butt of the Czech pistol in reply. I count the money while Morgan examines the pot, with honor satisfied on both sides. Jerry passes up the sail bag. Morgan counts the bricks. He nods in assent.

'Pleasure doing business, captain.'

'Safe journey,' he growls. 'If you're ever this way again, stop by.'

The moment I sit down, Jerry twists the throttle, spins the Zodiac, and races us away over the water. Behind us, I hear a bang. Turning around Morgan is waving his.45 Colt in a crazy pirate farewell.

Jerry slows to a sedate pace and tosses his gun into the bay.

'Why did you do that?'

'Who knows who heard that shot. Cash, we can explain. A gun is different.' He zips up his jacket against the wind. 'The first law of breaking the law is to only break one law at a time.'

After we pack the Zodiac away and put back all the requisitioned equipment, Jerry and I divvy up the spoils.

'One for you. One for me.' I say until two piles sit on the table.

'A plan well executed.' Jerry pays me back my original investment.

'Proper caper,' I reply, mimicking a crook from a black-and-white film. 'What are we going to do now?'

'Go and celebrate,' Jerry replies, off to stash his ill-gotten gains while I put mine under the mattress in the Coffin.

***

I'm feeling like my brain is being hit by a jackhammer as I hear the family returning. I'm currently sprawled on the settee in the main cabin and can't stand up.

'Where's my first mate?' Arno shouts. 'It's time to go!'

I sit up, sweaty and unkempt. Appearing first, Mickie stares at me.

'There's a note stuck to your face,' she says, peeling it off.

'What does it say?' I ask, unable to focus.

Mickie reads it out. SO LONG, and then a word I can't make out.

Oh, yes, it says, SO LONG FAGGOT!'

I grab the piece of paper from her hand and screw it up. All too soon, the first mate's vanishing act is clear to everyone.

'His things are gone,' Johanna says. 'Not even a note for me!'

Struggling to piece things together, I spot the empty bottle of rum and remember us drinking and getting a bit crazy. At some stage, I passed out; after that, Jerry abandoned ship.

'Who has been in my medicine chest?' Anna shouts.

Stumbling to the Coffin, I reach under the mattress—All my cash is gone. As the fuss over Jerry's disappearing act unfolds, I wake up to the fact that the bastard slipped me a Mickey Finn and did a runner.

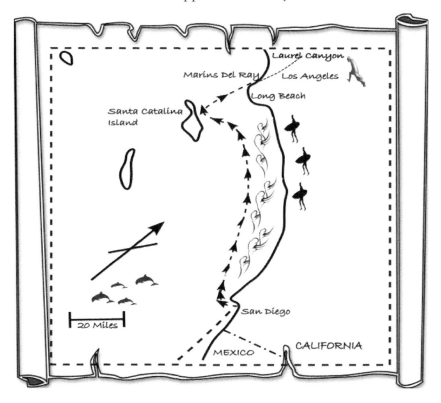

Chapter 10

Lover's Cove

Arno questions me about Jerry's sudden departure, I tread carefully. Telling the truth about Jerry's exit is not an option. Instead, I craft a tale of a tempting offer from a yacht heading south that may have poached him with a cash bribe. Oddly, Arno doesn't seem upset about his departure. Jerry did his job. We don't need protection now. And the Johanna issue is over. Conversely, what concerns Arno more than Jerry's departure is its timing. Jerry didn't wait to receive payment, which strikes the count as illogical. What's even more unusual is that Arno, typically a stickler for procedure, chooses not to report Jerry as absconding.

Anna says, 'I never like him. There is something in his eyes, a hint of mockery.' Jerry's absence shifts the dynamics onboard. In his pragmatic manner, Arno assigns the first mate's responsibilities and pay to me. 'But I need your word you'll come to Canada.'

'Don't leave us, Plum,' Lucie pleads. 'We need you.'

Her plea tugs at my heart, and financial realities force my hand. After a guarantee of a week's shore leave in San Francisco, I commit to the trip. Escaping the saloon, I retreat to the engine room. In the darkness, where I hid my hopes for the future, I break down. It wasn't the stash I couldn't trust—it was my partner.

Grappling with this setback, I recall *I Ching*'s counsel about 'not compromising with corruption.' I ignored the advice. The inevitable unfolded. I've no one but myself to blame.

Pulling myself together, I step out of the dark engine room into the brilliant Californian sunshine. To my surprise, Arno has gathered everyone on deck for a photograph with a new instant camera—the latest Polaroid SX-70, a nifty gadget that folds up small enough to fit in your pocket. The prospect of capturing instant memories is a bonus, especially considering that one film Anna took to the drugstore for processing didn't come out.

'Take a picture of us as a family group, will you, first mate,' Arno says, handing me the camera. Hearding them together to frame everyone in the shot, the resemblance between Johanna, Lucie, and Mickie becomes plain. They each bear a mix of their father's hauteur and their mother's warmth. As similar as peas in a pod, telling them apart will be challenge when Mickie grows up.

'Say cheese!' I shout, capturing the group photo. As the image develops, their faces reveal a momentary truth. The family tableau unfolds, showcasing a sardonic count, his stoic wife, the brittle Johanna, an obliging Lucie, and a mischievous Mickie. True to form, Mickie snatches the picture out of my hand, and they all huddle around, laughing in amazement at the instant artifact.

***

Under the guise of discussing a sailing strategy for the next leg of the journey, Lucie and I slip away for a drink and a bite at the clubhouse. However, our rendezvous doesn't go as planned.

'Why did Jerry make a quick exit?' Lucie's piercing blue eyes search my face for answers. 'You know more than you're letting on. What happened while we were away?'

'I've no idea,' I reply, sipping a much-needed beer to ease my hangover. 'All I remember from last night is having a few drinks in a bar, returning to the boat, and drinking rum. Jerry evidently slipped me something, and I passed out.'

'You didn't come-on to him, did you?' she asks, considering it a plausible scenario. 'And scare him off.'

'What gave you that idea?' I splutter into my beer.

'Well, what Jerry wrote on the note.'

'Faggot?'

'Yes! Mickie wanted to know what it meant.'

'What did you say?'

'That it's an English expression I don't understand.'

'No, I didn't come- on to Jerry. And what's more…'

'He told me he felt uncomfortable when you were alone. You had no idea he was leaving then?'.

I lean back, astounded by Jerry's deviousness but end up making an excuse for him. 'Because he wasn't allowed ashore, he seized the chance to jump ship when you were all away. I learned from a guy in the chandlery that he found a fishing charter boat heading south to Cabo San Lucas. Johanna's rejection had already taken its toll on his self-esteem, and the visa issue was the final straw.'

'Johanna, hosanna! Haven't you figured her out yet?' Lucie says, seemingly buying the story. 'She's Pavlov's dog around men—drooling. She needs them to want her. It's all about validation. Jerry was a guy to flirt with and string along. Anyway, she always fancied you more than him.'

'Me!' I exclaim. 'You must be joking.'

'If you weren't queer. Johanna would be all over you.'

Thrown off course by the comment, I determine to set the record straight. 'Lucie! Me being queer is something Jerry…'

'Plum, it's nothing to be ashamed of. It's what I like about you and why we're such good friends.'

Realizing it's pointless to try and correct her, I let it ride. Luckily Mickie interrupts our tête-à-tête and hustles an ice cream.

***

This morning, I refuse to let the gloomy weather dictate my mood. Jerry's gone, and now I'm the master of the deck. What I do from here on is what matters. Still, thoughts of Johanna fancying me linger. While I have no interest in her, the notion adds a touch of spice to the situation and might explain her demeanor.

'First mate, let go of the stern line,' Arno commands from the cockpit. As I coil the rope around my arm and tie it off, I notice Jerry's fishing rod on the taffrail, cursing him with a spiteful spit.

Arno charts our course for Los Angeles, home to movie stars, rock stars, cock stars, and fallen stars—all wishing on a star. Powering out of the bay, I'm relieved to leave San Diego behind— the city of my triumph in winning a deal and my downfall in losing it.

Lucie joins me at the pulpit rail as we navigate around Point Loma's kelp beds en route to Catalina Island. All of a sudden, we find ourselves amid a heated boat race. Power boats surge forth, skimming over the waves like skipping stones, more airborne than waterborne. Whipped by the high-speed wake, the sea fizzes and sprays assaulting us from every direction. It's a moment of motorized mayhem, akin to being in a swarm of wasps—here one minute, gone the next.

'Thank god that's over,' Lucie remarks as the trails of blue smoke vanish into the distance. I look at her in the sunshine, taken aback. She's sporting a pair of men's shorts, looking undeniably alluring. Then, I recognize them. 'They're mine!' I exclaim.

'Oh, my gosh!' she feigns surprise, peering down at the faded blue cutoffs secured with a sail tie. 'I wondered whose they were. They were in the laundry bag. I thought Jerry had left them behind.'

No, you didn't, I think. *I wore those on the beach when we were collecting clams.* Looking at her expression of feigned innocence I feel a delightful ticklish sensation inside.

No sooner do we escape one noisy nightmare than we plunge into another. Hours later, we sail under the Los Angeles International Airport flight path, and the sky transforms into a murky yellow. Planes take off at regular intervals, and I duck in reflex. The Pan Am 747 roaring overhead is the loudest noise I've ever heard. Lucie covers her ears and retreats down the deck. I follow suit.

'Don't worry,' Arno says as we join him and Mickie in the cockpit. 'This is the wrong side of the tracks. We're not here long.'

'What do you mean?' Mickie looks puzzled. 'There are no tracks.'

'It's crazy how something as simple as railroad tracks can divide a community so sharply,' Arno says, shaking his head.

Between planes, Arno explains that when they built the railroads, the tracks became a demarcation line.

'Like a barrier between two different worlds.' I pipe in.

Arno nods. 'Exactly! Depending on which way the wind blew the locomotive smoke, people ended up living on either the 'right' or the 'wrong' side. And that decided a lot about their lives.'

'Yeah,' I pipe in. 'On one side, people pay the police to keep out the riffraff to assure real estate values and live the American Dream.'

'But on the other side,' Arno continues, 'life was much tougher. People had to fight for everything to survive.'

Mickie thinks about this for a moment. 'But that's not fair. People shouldn't be judged or treated differently based on where they live or how much money they have.'

Arno smiles, proud of her insight. 'You're right, Mickie. It's not fair. But that's the way life is.'

Skulking off, Mickie goes below to think about it. Lucie gives me a better-go-check-look and follows her.

Wanting to check our position, Arno hands me the helm, leaving me in command. Overcoming the stinging sensation in my eyes caused by the plane exhaust, this is a moment to relish. I am now a professional sailor, on a path that could lead me to become a skipper.

***

It's mid-afternoon when I step onto the deck and head to the stern, seeking fresh air. Someone is following me. I turn around, *Click*, a Polaroid emerges from the camera Johanna's purloined from Arno. She's in a bikini and presses the film against her breast to speed development before peeling it away with a laugh.

'You're so camp in your off-the-shoulder alpaca sweater, with your golden tresses and cupid bow lips,' she remarks.

'Wow!' I exclaim, shocked at the image, not having seen myself for months. 'It's not my natural style.'

'Must be a man in there somewhere,' she says handing me the camera. 'Go on, take a picture of me.'

She reclines on the afterdeck and strikes a pose. While I'm setting up the shot, Lucie appears from below. She's clearly put out by the scene. 'What's happening here?'

'Glamour snaps,' I say, realizing too late how wrong it sounds.

Without a word, Lucie turns and walks away.

Johanna lifts her sunglasses and smiles. 'She's always been jealous of my beauty. I can't help it if you find me attractive.'

'You're trying to stir things up now that Jerry's gone.'

'Well, I suppose you're better than nothing,' she says, placing a wrist against her forehead. 'I'm so lonesome I could cry.'

***

Santa Monica Bay curves along the Southern California coast. We find ourselves amidst a flotilla of yachts racing to Catalina Island. Navigating the transition from power to sail requires a vigilant lookout and nimble maneuvering to dodge the swanky sailboats. Arno decides to go with the flow, charting a course to Catalina, our destination for the night, before heading to the mainland tomorrow.

Lucie returns to her element with the opportunity to sail again, coming to life the moment we raise some canvas. Her adeptness at catching the wind is no surprise, capturing my heart in the process. The sight of her bare, bronzed arms trimming the jib sheet reveals a woman using her skill to conquer powerful forces—an opposite approach to Johanna, who employs her wiles to toy with men. With Lucie, it's as though we don't exist.

The sea becomes choppy as the afternoon progresses. However, the light breeze helps keep the bumps at bay, allowing us to make good progress as we sail past Surf City—the very place that inspired the Beach Boys' famous songs about curling waves, longboards, and sun-kissed bodies. It's where freedom-loving boomers live, believing that a bad day surfing is better than a good day working.

The wind and our sails ease as we arrive at Catalina Island. The glow of lights from the mainland reflects on the clouds, creating an artificial atmosphere as we enter Lover's Cove. We secure a mooring for an overnight stay by a Chinese junk lying at anchor.

After launching the tender, Mickie, Lucie and I go ashore to buy lobsters. Tying up to a wooden jetty, we explore a mini village of garishly painted restaurants, souvenir shops, and market stalls. While

Mickie grabs a snow cone, Lucie and I haggle with a vendor for live crustaceans lying torpid in a large glass tank. She plops the creatures into a bubbling cauldron using long-handled tongs.

'You are a good-looking couple,' she says as the creatures cook.

Lucie and I exchange glances and laugh in embarrassment.

'No! No!' Lucie says, dismissing the notion. 'That's ridiculous.'

'Trust me, you are. You can only pretend for so long!'

'Glad we're convincing,' I say. 'We're working undercover.'

'And I'm Edgar Hoover,' she replies unconvinced.

Trailing a rich, briny smell of freshly boiled lobster, we stroll back, with Mickie in a buffer zone between us. When a jukebox plays "Lyin' Eyes" by the Eagles the hot hit of '75, she tugs my pants.

'They play music so you can't hear the lobsters scream as they die.'

Lucie laughs 'She only said it to put me off eating them.'

'You got it in one,' the rascal snickers. 'All the more for me.'

Back at base, Mickie is up and aboard in a flash, followed by Lucie, whose legs brush my face as I hold the tender steady. Anna lets out a whoop when she empties the creatures into the galley sink. After examining the shells and checking that their tails curl under their bodies, she splits each with a hefty cleaver. Rather than make anything fancy, Anna extracts all the flesh, mixes it with mayo and lemon juice, splits hot dog buns in half, and dishes up lobster rolls.

Everyone gathers in the cockpit, drooling. We devour the food as though we haven't eaten for a week. Mickie then parades around with a pair of claws, pretending to be Lobster Woman, the crazy crustacean. I fight her off with a fork. Johanna clears up by dropping all the shells over the side and clapping her hands in a done-and-dusted gesture before the girls go below.

'What will you do with *Hoop* once you're back?' I ask Arno.

'We have to make it home first,' he replies, neatly deflecting the question. Anna is pragmatic. 'We need to return to normal life first.'

'But what's normal? You'll all have changed so much,' I say. 'How can you go back to the same old, same old?'

Arno laughs. 'I have some advice for you, Plum. When you return home, and you will, people might not notice much of a change in you. So don't waste your time trying to prove to them how much you've grown.' He notices the disappointment on my face. 'It's harsh but you know you had the time of your life. You can't relive those moments; they're gone. Remember, you are more than your memories, and move on.'

***

In the morning, as Arno and I haul the tender on deck, I tell him about the times we've been at anchor when I've heard shrimp nibbling at the growth on the hull. Sometimes, I've also heard muffled noises of fish banging against the keel. But last night, I heard an eerie, wailing sound that came from everywhere and nowhere.

The count gives me a knowing look. 'Nay,' he says before explaining the phenomenon. '*Hoop* was built in the Baltic. What you heard is the *Klabautermann*, a sprite who protects this boat. But it's a good thing you didn't see him.'

'Why?' I ask, intrigued that the ever-rational Arno serves up folklore before breakfast.

He pauses for a moment, then whispers, 'The story goes, if you ever set eyes on the *Klabautermann*, it means doom for the ship.'

'Nothing to worry about then,' I say light-heartedly.

'On the contrary,' Arno has an otherworldly look in his eyes. 'From now on, we must be extra vigilant because he's ensuring we're ready for the last part of the trip. When it's over, it will change everything, restore the old order, make things whole again.' Then adds as an afterthought. 'Tell no one you heard him. It's our secret.'

Nodding, I humor the count, thinking he's pulling my leg. However, I can't shake off Arno's earlier advice at the beginning of the voyage, urging me always to take him seriously. The idea of the fabled *Klabautermann* being a crew member is intriguing; what other secrets lie hidden in the hull?

***

After casting off from the mooring and waving goodbye to Catalina Island, Lucie and I hoist the genoa to a pleasant northwest breeze and set sail forty-two miles to the mainland.

By late afternoon, after a glorious day's sailing, Arno lets the Coast Guard know a foreign-registered vessel is coming in. Below is a flurry in the aft cabin in anticipation of spacious showers ashore. Back on deck, I spot the beacon on the south jetty guiding us into Marina del Rey, where the plan is to prep for the run to San Francisco.

The Del Rey Yacht Club is so modern, bright, and white that it could be a bank. Boats of every description are in the slips, from the late Humphrey Bogart's schooner *Santana* to an ex-Coast Guard patrol boat converted into a cabin cruiser. When we dock at a guest berth, *Hoop* appears to all the world the difference between a hobby and a way of life.

The membership secretary gives us a friendly welcome and signs us in. Arno's *Seven Seas Sailing Association* burgee entitles us to use all facilities, including a beauty salon that the girls are quick to take advantage of. Once alone, I wander about the clubhouse, drinking from an ice-cool water fountain and gazing into a vending machine full of fizzy pop and candy. On reading the notice board, I feel envious of the West Coast way of life. The weekends are full of races, and regattas. The club's membership policy is open to anyone. A place geared up for a lifestyle I've only seen on the TV.

Watching the girls appear from the pampering department, I compliment Lucie on her hairdo, which adds polish to her 'barefoot contessa' image. 'Glad you noticed,' she says, twirling. 'You don't think they've taken too much off, do you?'

'That style suits you,' I say.

'What about mine?' Johanna says with a hint of envy.

***

Leaving Mickie to giggle at the girls' hairdos, Arno, Anna, and I go for supper in the club. As the final days of their journey together unfold, a palpable tension begins to weave between them—tonight, I'm the buffer zone. The air-conditioned restaurant has a dress code.

Anna's in a dated blouse and slacks, me in my linen suit, and Arno in a Tyrolean jacket. We attract curious glances from other patrons.

Not long after we sit down than someone at the bar takes offense at Arno's German accent. In a loud voice for us to hear, a short, well-built man wearing a Star of David lapel pin says to his two friends, 'When I was stationed there after the war, not one Nazi ever came up and said, I'm sorry.' Then, turning to lean on the bar and face us, he continues, 'The Krauts all claimed they were following orders.'

'I didn't think,' Anna whispers. 'They allowed Jews in yacht clubs.'

'This one is different,' I say, shocked by her. 'Jewish sailboat racers founded this as their place, as other clubs wouldn't let them join.'

'There are half a million of us living here that you bastards missed,' the man at the bar shouts, unembarrassed and unashamed.

Arno puts down his menu and walks over to him 'Sir, I was ten when Germany invaded Czechoslovakia. The Nazis murdered thousands who resisted. After the war, the Communists took over. I lost everything and fled to Canada, penniless. Regarding your people, there's nothing for which I must apologize. Now, please allow us to enjoy our meal.' His chutzpah quietens the men at the bar, and staring at the menu, I wonder if I've witnessed an exhibition of blue blood hauteur or—as Arno told me that he spent the last days of the war in Vienna, not Prague—my first encounter with Holocaust denial.

'Now, where were we?' Arno says. 'I'll have the matzoh ball soup.'

Chapter II

Queen Bee

Sailors like to catch the tide, feel the wind and spin a yarn, so a marina's always buzzing with gossip. This morning, Arno, now accepted as a blue-water sailor rather than an old enemy, is up and down the jetty talking to everyone and anyone. Anna, meanwhile, not to be outdone by her daughters, has dragged Mickie off to the beauty salon. This leaves Johanna and Lucie, all bare flesh and suntan lotion, sunning themselves on deck while I check out the yachts heading off for a day's racing. They tease me about scoping out the men onboard. 'I might be interested in the boats,' I shoot back.

'Gawd! What wouldn't I give to be rich,' pines Johanna, trying to look like Jackie-O in her wraparounds.

'What's to become of us, Plum?' Lucie asks, sounding stupefied. 'Are we doomed to die of boredom?'

The racing boats disappear, leaving us to swelter in the California heat, and a sense of boredom washes over us—something never felt at sea where every day brings new challenges, and you don't have a sense of missing out. The hot sunny afternoon stretches on endlessly. The minutes tick by. We yearn for something to break the monotony. Finally, relief arrives as a schooner boasting teak decks, bronze fittings, and masts that reach the heavens, ties up beside us and blocks out the sun.

Johanna is quick to voice her frustration. 'As lovely as your boat is, it's messing up our chance at a tan, and trust me, we don't have much else on the agenda.'

Two crew secure the boat and strut down the gangway, dressed in a kaleidoscope of tie-dye and double denim. One is David Crosby, the singer-songwriter of "Wooden Ships".

'I'll tell you what,' he says, a beatific smile cracking beneath his walrus moustache. 'Let me play you a song I've written. If your nipples perk up, I'll tell the sun to spin on a different axis.'

'That's a strange request, stranger,' Johanna says.

'A sure-fire way of telling if it's a hit.'

'Strum on then, troubadour,' she says, sitting up all prepared as our new neighbour launches into a ballad to which his friend sings sweet harmony.

We all stare at Johanna's T-shirt and notice the magic happen.

'One for the next album,' I say, applauding.

'You guys want to come to a party tonight?'

Johanna leans over, flirting, 'Let me check with my people. Plum! Are we busy tonight?'

'No, countess, we've cancelled drinks on deck due to a lack of ice.'

With twinkling wizard eyes, our host-to-be whispers, 'Be ready by seven. My limo will come and take you all to heaven.'

He disappears up the jetty, the girls are beside themselves.

'You know who that is,' Lucie says, blown away.

'Dave Crosby's invited me to a party,' Johanna simpers.

'Must be your new look,' I say, amused by her preening. Although it's easy to tell why she got asked. The sisters are not your regular Cali girls but captivating beauties of another time and place!

'Oh, we must go. We've got to go!' both squeal in unison.

Trying to calm them down, I say, 'Let's not get ahead of ourselves. If you ask your parents if you can party with a load of drug-crazed rock stars, what will they say?'

They don't even try to reply, as the answer is obvious.

'You've got two options. Sneak out or spin a cover story.'

'Sneak out,' Johanna jumps up and down, her breasts bouncing.

'What's the story?' Lucie asks.

'Leave that to me. But those guys were high—who knows if they'll remember to send the car.'

Arno and Anna offer no resistance when I suggest taking Johanna and Lucie to the cinema.

'One of the yacht club members is an investor in a movie and has left preview tickets for anyone to take,' I say. 'It's called *The Rocky Horror Picture Show*, and it's showing at a theatre on Sunset Strip.'

'We could all go,' says Anna.

'You'd hate it.' I say heading her off at the pass. 'It's a spoof sci-fi comedy film of a musical I saw in London. Lots of loud music and not suitable for children.'

In a huff, Mickie folds her arms. 'At least bring back popcorn.'

'Don't wait up for us,' I say breezily to buy us some more party time. 'We'll hang out on the Strip and soak up the atmosphere.'

***

'That's a bit overdressed for the movies,' Arno comments when Johanna comes in all dolled up in a mid-length muslin prairie dress and makeup.

'Papa don't be such a square. A film director might spot me and give me a part in a Hollywood blockbuster. I'll become an overnight sensation and restore the family fortune.'

'Bet she only makes it to the casting couch,' quips Lucie, radiant in a rainbow-striped tube top, hipster jeans and cool clogs.

The joke draws a disapproving glance from her mother. 'You behave yourselves. I don't know who's worse,' Anna scolds.

I'm wearing my white linen suit and green silk shirt, which is classy enough to get in any joint.

We head off arm in arm to the club forecourt, looking like we're brother and sisters and me, the luckiest guy alive.

Parked between a Lincoln Continental coupe and a Cadillac Eldorado cabriolet, a silver 1950s Bentley Continental awaits us, looking timeless yet contemporary. I open the door pretending to be a footman, and the girls step in as though to the manner born. We slide into the plush leather seats enveloped in a cocoon of comfort. Lounging in back of the limo, I catch the driver's gaze in the rearview mirror. A knowing look in his eyes rings a warning bell. It's as if we're part of the film we should be watching.

'Oh, I say,' a cut-glass English voice exclaims from the passenger seat as a pocket-rocket in her mid-twenties turns round to face us. 'You are a perfect pair,' she says, a floppy velvet cap sitting atop a mischievous face.

'Now you're in the time-ship, let's rip. I'm Bee, he's Percy.'

Turning the Bakelite-rimmed steering wheel with the leather palm of his Chester Jefferies gloves, Percy circles the Bentley off the forecourt onto a palm-fringed boulevard. We swish away from the ocean and swiggity-swag our way up winding roads to the Hollywood hills. The bright lights of passing cars illuminate the girls' faces, drop-jawed at their good fortune.

'This is surreal,' Lucie says. 'But I like it.'

'You'll become used to it, darling,' says Bee, kneeling on the seat for a better view.

'Where are we going?' Johanna asks, excited by whatever's in store.

'We're going to a party.'

Lucie asks for more information. 'Whose party?'

Bee feigns surprise. 'The person putting on the party.'

'Who's that?' I ask, confused.

'Absolutely no idea, darling.' Bee turns to the driver. 'Percy, dear, whose party, is it?'

The eyes in the rearview mirror flicker with exasperation. 'Tonight's the night,' As though it's a riddle. 'Tonight's the night.'

'Oh, yes,' Bee says blithely. 'Someone's launching an album.'

'Who?' Lucie asks.

'No idea,' Bee says with a smile. 'The Coz called and told us to come and collect you.'

'Is this what you do?' Johanna asks, clearly intrigued by what's going on. 'Like a job?'

Bee explains that Percy had the limo shipped from England. Together, they ferry rock and film stars and their entourages to premieres and parties all over LA. She's a must-have fixture related to British royalty. Her nickname is "Queen Bee".

'We're royalty too,' Insists Johanna. 'Countesses from Bohemia.'

'Then, my pea-perfect darlings, you're made. There'll be buckets of bohemians where we're going.'

'Any Transylvanians?' I ask. Percy lets out a sinister laugh.

'What will we have to do?' Johanna senses an opportunity.

'You flit amongst the in-crowd, sprinkling the fairy dust of majesty. Stars want to touch the hem of your garment to believe they're in heaven.' Bee crosses herself at her near blasphemy.

'But we don't have any money,' Johanna says.

'You have what money can't buy!'

'What's that?'

'Class!' Percy says, pointing out Beverly Hills to our left. 'You can buy style but can't buy class, so they rent it from us by the hour.'

We cross over Cadillac Avenue and make our way up Laurel Canyon Boulevard, heading into the Santa Monica Mountains, the scent of jasmine fills the car. Percy calls it the *flower of the gods*. Sitting next to Lucie, with her sun-kissed skin radiating vitality and stray strands of tousled hair dancing in the breeze, intoxication takes on a new meaning. This strange journey has all the makings of a night to remember. As Frank-N-Furter says, 'Don't dream it, be it.'

***

Percy sweeps us up a driveway, spins the car in a shower of gravel, and parks in front of a Gothic-style mansion for a quick getaway.

'Let's get you people party prepped,' Bee says, leaning over with a silver spoon piled high with glistening white crystals. 'You girls are going to shine tonight.'

'What's that?' Lucie asks as Johanna leans forward and sniffs the powder up one slender nostril.

'What they don't put in Coca-Cola anymore.' Bee reloads the spoon and almost shoves it up Lucie's nose. Refusing the temptation she recoils. Bee offers it to me. I take in one hefty snort. After taking the hit, I feel a surge of alertness and energy. That's when I notice Percy staring at me through rearview mirror eyes. Overtaken by a sudden grandiosity, I quip, 'Not indulging, driver?'

'*Adsum servire, mi princeps.*' With the enigmatic comment hanging in the air, he exits the car and slips on a pink jacket with a kiddie's sheriff's badge pinned on the lapel. Then, he opens the limousine's rear door, gesturing for us to step out with a theatrical bow and a sweep of his arm. His mocking smile warns that this isn't the first time he's delivered lambs to the slaughter. But it's too late to back out now, and with the drugs kicking in, I feel invincible.

Bee looks boyish and cute, dressed in hot pants, knee-high boots, and a fringed suede top, like a pixie enticer. We follow her through the vast oak doors into a sea of 'anything goes' party people, all gawking to glimpse the new arrivals. The air is heavy with smoke and musty perfume. We step into a fever dream. A world where rules don't apply.

While I take it all in, Bee introduces 'her countesses' to a cool skinny dude in a velvet jacket, studded belt and winkle-picker shoes, who at once hits on Johanna. Squinting through the viewfinder of a Polaroid, he takes close-ups. She pouts at the camera while shooing us away.

'Johanna's hot to trot,' I say as Lucie slips her arm into mine.

'Escort me, Plum. Pretend you're a dashing naval officer. I want to feel like it's the old days at a glittering ball in Vienna, and I'm a countess coming out in public for the first time.'

We walk through large rooms with ornate fireplaces, questionable art, and kitsch. We are at a party where glamour, excess, and recklessness are plated like canapes.

Bee, appearing out of nowhere with a guy sporting a disarming smile, introduces him to Lucie, 'You simply must meet each other. With your royal connections, you would be a great addition to his close circle of intimate friends.'

She grabs me by my arm. 'Young man, you can't monopolize our charming countess all night. You're cramping her style.'

Distracted by a band tuning up, I leave Lucie to fend for herself and bustle into a courtyard where a group of musicians tune up for an impromptu jam session. The crowd cheers as the jam band launches into a freewheeling improvisation. All eyes are glued to the stage as the musos trade solos and harmonize with each other. The atmosphere's intoxicating, a heady mix of fame, talent, and the thrill of being in the midst of it all. It should be a night to remember, a moment of pure magic only Hollywood can provide, until I realize the songs are pretentious twaddle about musicians taking too many drugs, knowing their once seemingly indestructible bodies are starting to give out. I have the impression that the good times aren't so good anymore. Though I want to enjoy myself, I can't.

I look around for the girls, but all I see are sleazy zombies. Pills and hard booze are everywhere. The atmosphere has a nasty edge. In a moment of clarity, I realize I'm here five years too late—the dream is over, and I need to wake up. Feeling guilty about leaving Lucie alone like a honey pot for a hungry bear to find, I worm my way through the revellers.

On my way out, I bump into a *Muscle Mary* who spits in my face when I brush off his come-on with a tart one-liner. The shock wakes me, and aware of the time, I set out to hunt for the girls. I find Lucie by the pool, sitting under a colossal eucalyptus, looking dejected. I drape my jacket over her shoulders.

'What happened to you?' I ask, sitting down next to her.

'I wanted the party to be fun. But everyone here is so false. After you abandoned me, that asshole tried to screw me. When I put up a fight and knee him in the crotch, the slimeball shouted at me that I was a stuck-up prick-tease and should forget about ever working in this town.'

'I shouldn't have left you. Bee dragged me away.'

'Yes, the little bitch set me up. She's a madam for these creatures, delivering them fresh meat.'

'Sorry, Lucie, for letting you down.'

'Oh Plum, becoming a woman is so scary. It's like standing on thin ice and hearing the surface crack.' Her words taper away as she flings her arms around me for a reassuring hug. 'Can't we go, Plum? Let's go home.'

Finally, I gather the courage and want to kiss her.

'That's why I feel safe with you,' she says, oblivious to my intention. 'You're kind and…'

'Stay here, Lucie.' I put her down like a treasure I can't afford. 'I'll go and find Johanna.'

'She's in the pool house,' Lucie says. 'There's an orgy going on.'

***

The smell of the cabin is overwhelmingly pungent and musky. Treading carefully through the body-strewn room, I spot Johanna's unmistakable naked bum on a bed and the photographer, with his 'let's check if the camera likes you' gambit, fully dressed but passed out in a chair beside her.

'Johanna, wake up,' I say, shaking her. 'It's time to go.'

Pushing me away with the disdain you'd show for a dirty dishcloth, she gets up and slips on her dress. Several Polaroids are scattered among the bedsheets, and I scoop them up as she tiptoes to the door. Outside, she shoots me a 'that was fun, glad it's all over' look while pulling on her shoes.

With Lucie clutching my jacket tightly and Johanna stumbling behind, only half awake, we search for Percy.

After a while, his pink jacket gives him away, but he's lying on a hammock in a haze of a heroin high. I ask him about returning to the boat, but dilated pupils stare back at me as black as Blind Pew's spot, and his reply is unintelligible gibberish.

'Seems we're on our own.' With a girl on each arm, so I don't lose them, we form a human chain and search for a way out of the labyrinth, where every room leads to another. Finally, we find ourselves in a large games room where a rowdy group is engaged in a lively game of pool. The air resounds with the clack of balls as alpha males play shots and hustle for big bucks. As we circle the room for the exit, Johanna whispers the names of the famous faces.

'Leaving with two at once,' one dude says, smashing the eight-ball home. 'That's greedy.'

They say you should never meet your heroes—particularly if you're wired and the cocaine devil's up to making mischief.

'Go fuck yourself, grasshopper,'

A hush falls over the room as all eyes turn on the TV icon, and he's not about to play the bamboo flute.

'No one, you English motherfucker,' David Carradine spits the words at me, 'calls me that and lives to tell the tale.'

Vaulting onto the pool table, cue in hand, he twirls it like a bō staff. In a flash, the atmosphere turns ugly, and I'm the bad guy in an episode of *Kung Fu* with Kwai Chang Caine hovering above me praying mantis style. Tension hangs thick in the air. Then, an ominous creak, an unsettling crack, and a precarious wobble as the table collapses, sending him crashing to the floor. As he sprawls, spreadeagled in a tangle of broken wood and spilt drinks, there's a moment of stunned silence, followed by shouting and confusion. I grab the girls and run.

Hurrying outside, pumped up on fear and adrenaline, I spot the Bentley pointing downhill. It's our getaway car. I bundle the girls in the back, hop in and release the handbrake. We freewheel off the driveway. The gods are with us. Percy left the key in the ignition. With the engine on, we spiral downhill towards the city lights and the dark arc of the coastline.

With no word said between us, I guide the car down the winding, jasmine-scented roads. The drive is a blur, but dawn breaks as we pull into the marina, and relief washes over me. The night's terrors are banished, and we've made it back. However, we've traded one trouble for another.

Arno is waiting outside the clubhouse, arms akimbo. We clamber out of the car, all tired eyes and ragged, guilty smiles, his face is a unique expression of relief and disbelief. 'How was the film?' he asks. 'And why back so late?'

'We missed it, so we went to the live show instead,' I reply, groping for an alibi. 'It went on longer than expected.'

'It was further away too,' Lucie adds for good measure.

'We got lost on the way back' Johanna contributes to the fiction.

Arno shakes his head as the girls scurry past, looking dishevelled and wearing matching sheepish grins. He sighs, knowing they are pushing the boundaries and testing his patience again. He is relieved that they are back safe and doesn't scold me but runs his fingers over the graceful lines of the Bentley as if it evokes memories. 'While we have the use of a limousine, Anna wants stop by the grocery store.'

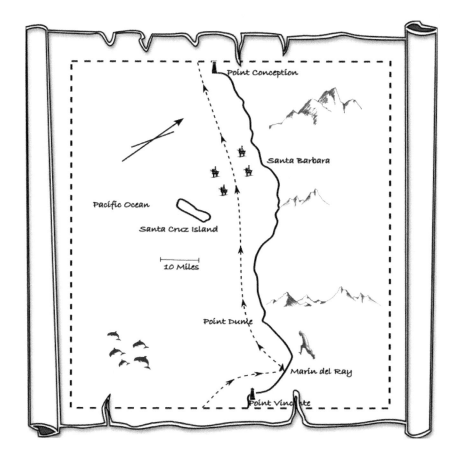

Chapter 12

Obeying Orders

With our provisions fully stocked, I leave the keys to the Bentley with the club secretary and a brief note for Percy and head back to *Hoop* to wait for Arno's familiar cry of 'Let go of the bow line'.

By late afternoon, we're in the Santa Barbara Channel and spot a gas burn-off from an offshore oil rig's flare stack. The flames soaring high against the misty sky appear otherworldly from a distance. Yet as we enter the oilfield, more rigs become visible; a harsh reality asserts itself when, along with a constant mechanical clanking noise, a slick of oil appears on the water's surface and the air reeks of rotten eggs. Small supply vessels scuttle back and forth between the platforms, their captains unconcerned as they cut across our bow at top speed.

While Mickie shouts warnings from the rigging, the other girls are look-outs on the side rails. Arno is on radar duty, scanning for hazards while I steer us through the chaos, afraid the oil in the water may affect the engine's cooling system. It's a tense time all around as Anna's worried that the petrochemicals will ruin the paintwork. By nightfall, the worst is behind us, and with the clouds glowing red from the burn-offs, the place resembles the 'Sack of Rome'. When Arno takes the wheel, he tells me that only half a barrel of oil produces gasoline; the rest goes to ink, tires, and asphalt but increasingly to the production of plastic.

'Plastics!' He pauses for effect. 'There's a great future in plastics.'

However smart the prediction from *The Graduate* may be, the present asserts itself as a small boat bursts out of the flickering gloom, and dashes across our bow. All we hear is the boisterous laughter of riggers looking forward to shore leave after weeks of hard work and long hours.

By midnight, we're clear of the toxic chaos and are motoring in a flat calm as the wind has dropped completely. Shorthanded since Jerry's departure, Anna now takes a spell on watch with Arno. For over a year, the sea has been their escape, where they left the humdrum behind. Yet as they return home, the vast ocean reflects their growing distance. Terse exchanges now punctuate the once harmonious days at sea as long-simmering resentments surface. They're silent tonight as we head towards the Cojo anchorage east of Point Conception.

Climbing in the Coffin, I find my linen suit trousers crumpled in the corner where I had tossed them before setting sail. The Polaroid pictures I picked up at the party are still in my pocket. They depict a shockingly exotic tale. After tucking them under the mattress, I drift into an erotic dream as entangled as the bodies in the photographs.

***

The Coffin felt cramped when we were down south, but it feels cosy now that it's getting colder. Before, I was out as soon as I woke up, but now I linger until the last minute.

Idling in bed this morning, I shuffle through photos that would make a sailor blush. They are pictures of Johanna, caught in innocent and downright dirty poses. First, the countess arrives at the party. Then, in the poolside cabin, with hands where they shouldn't be. And lastly, in the throes of pleasure, entwined with the gamine little Bee. Quick as a cat, I hide the steamy snapshots lest the prying eyes of the *Klabautermann* catch wind of them. After which I flee the Coffin.

On deck, Lucie at the helm. I avoid eye contact lest mine betray what I've been looking at, so I hurry to the foredeck for anchor duty as we arrive.

Sandy bluffs, tufted with sea grass, ring a sheltered bay. The only signs of civilization are railroad telegraph lines running behind a beach of brown sand. Avoiding the thick kelp beds that could entangle the propellers, we navigate towards clear waters and drop anchor thirty yards from the shore.

After dinner, Mickie brings out a deck of cards, and we play Old Maid using a standard deck with the Queen of Clubs removed. I'm sitting between Johanna and Lucie, so I must take a card from one and offer my hand to the other. It is a unique form of exquisite torment. On the one hand, I look at the face of a woman I've seen in flagrante delicto, while on the other sits the one for whom I yearn. Johanna's comments couldn't be more predictable when I'm left holding the last card.

Cast as the lonely queen, I bid everyone goodnight and head to the Coffin to work out what to do with the pictures. It would be sensible to destroy them, but you can't easily tear up Polaroids. If I throw them out the porthole, they might still be floating in the morning. I hide them away; aware I am now sleeping on a time bomb.

***

With only the mizzen sail hoisted as a riding sail to help stabilize the boat, we set out early after a stark briefing from Arno. 'Point Conception is known as the Cape Horn of the Pacific,' he says. 'It's nicknamed the Graveyard.'

With the engines vibrating beneath us, I turn to Arno. 'Sometimes, skipper, I wonder why you ever started this journey.'

Arno holds my gaze. 'Fortune Favours the Bold.'

'More *Rheingold*?'

'No! Virgil.' With a knowing chortle, Arno revs up the engines to drown our conversation, leaving me none the wiser.

The sea has laid down overnight, and Arno wants to put as many miles behind us as possible before the early afternoon northwest wind picks up. In the relative calm, we make good speed beneath a mackerel sky, slipping past Point Conception lighthouse at first light. This is where the Santa Barbara Channel meets the open Pacific Ocean, a natural boundary between Southern and Central California, heralding a change in the weather and the people. Now we're heading north; morality clamps up in the cold. I've got a sense it now will not play well if the girls call me out as bent when we're ashore, as gay pride never got further than Haight Ashbury. I decide it's time to put an end to this myth.

Twelve miles on, we round Point Arguello, another prominent crag with its portfolio of disaster stories. Today, it's relatively benign, with waves building up without breaking. These pose no problems as I steer us around the bluff. We're almost clear when Anna comes on deck with the binoculars.

'What are you looking for?' I ask.

'It's hard to believe, but on those fearsome rocks, seven US destroyers followed one another to their destruction in 1928.'

'Why?' Curious to know how it happened.

'The six captains following the admiral were obeying orders.'

After my afternoon watch, I meet Johanna alone on the foredeck, listening to her transistor radio. Still out of kilter from my private viewing, I can't help mentioning the Polaroids.

'I've something to tell you,' I say, kneeling beside her, all too aware of the curves of her body, which I now know too well.

'What about?' she says, reluctantly turning down the transistor playing "Rock the Boat", a feel-good disco song.

'No, keep it up. I don't want anyone to hear.'

'OK, Mr. Mysterious, spill the beans.'

'Remember at the party when I came to find you in the cabin?'

Johanna shifts uneasily. 'I was pretty high that night.'

'Well, some pictures were scattered about.'

'The photographer was poking his camera everywhere,' she says.

'Well, I picked them up.'

'Let me look!' she says, reaching out.

'They're hidden away. But you wouldn't want anyone else on board to see them.'

'Are they naughty?' She blushes.

'Yes! One in particular.'

'Oh, my god, Plum,' she says, all excited 'Listen, you're the only one I can tell this to. And since you're gay, I won't feel uncomfortable about it. When the photographer took me into the cabin, naughty things were happening. Bee started kissing me. By this time, I was so horny that I didn't mind. Let me tell you, she knew how to get me off faster than any guy has.' Johanna stretches her arms above her head and arches her back. 'I didn't feel like a countess, I was a queen.'

'And it was all caught on camera.'

'Was I enjoying myself?'

'Oh, yes.'

'I want them,' she says impatiently, then adds, 'and Lucie must never find out about Bee.'

While I promise to keep what Johanna calls 'our naughty little secret,' Lucie spots us and asks what's happening.

'I was telling Plum about Jerry's dick.'

Lucie looks at me, surprised. 'I told you already.'

'Yes! But I can never hear it enough.'

She's not convinced. 'You two are up to something.'

Chapter 13

No Peeking

By late afternoon, the weather changes, and ominous clouds obscure the snow-capped mountains along the coast. The wind picks up at sea level, and the current against us grows more potent. *Hoop* is moving at a sluggish pace simply to make headway. I pop to check how the engines are coping with the extra workload.

The engine room is warm after the cold of the open cockpit but it's noisy. The human ear is a sensitive organ that can induce emotional responses, and engine noise is no exception. A chukka, chukka, chukka sewing machine sound means all is well. So long as I keep oil in the crankcase and air out of the fuel line, Dick and Harry are a pair of optimists, all guts and heart. But something is amiss.

Perkins engines don't often complain, but Dick has started to bleat. To find the source of the problem, I use a long-shanked screwdriver as a stethoscope, pressing my ear to the handle while placing the tip on the engine block. A loud and persistent grinding noise is coming from the drive shaft. I must tell the skipper at once as the bearing is running hot.

'We'll take sick Dick down to slow revs to keep his prop moving and hope we can press on with Harry,' he replies with habitual pragmatism. 'The surf will stop us from getting into Carmel Bay. We'll have to fix it in San Francisco.'

'How will that affect the handling?'

'We've a danger of slowly drifting off course. The good thing is we don't have far to go.'

While the sun falls towards the horizon, we progress steadily along the California coast. In the background, there's the roar of waves crashing against rocks. The wind whips up sheets of spray from the cold blue tumult, leaving a tang of salt on my tongue. The Point Sur lighthouse, atop a massive rock, is a focal point of the dying light. Next to it, high on the edge of the cliffs, perches the Esalen Institute.

Two years before, my American friend Bob took me to this Shangri-La of the Counterculture to hear Alan Watts, the English philosopher, preach the Religion of No-Religion. His was a Zen Buddhist pop philosophy for people who dislike organized religion but believe there's a spiritual realm as well as a mortal one. Bob and I lapped up Watts's intriguing aphorisms. He described himself as part monk, part huckster—a character I would like to emulate.

High on the memory, the colours of the day fade away as we enter nautical twilight—the mystical moment when the horizon and stars are both visible. Alphecca shines bright in the constellation of the Northern Crown, almost beckoning me to shine my light and illuminate the world, and right now, I believe I can. As the dark wraps us in its shroud, tentacles of phosphorescence dance in our wake, creating an otherworldly magic that's impossible to ignore.

Before midnight, when I finish my watch, Johanna comes up on deck and stands close behind me. I feel myself tingling, excited by her proximity and the intimacy of her voice whispering in my ear, 'When can I have the pictures?'

'Well, I can't hand them to you at breakfast. Let's wait till tomorrow when we're in San Francisco.'

Johanna whispers that she'll put a book on my bunk to hide the Polaroids. I then ask her to wake Lucie for her watch.

'She won't be asleep for wondering about our little secret.' A wicked smile flickers across her face. 'Lucie hates deception.'

'You're a piece of work, Johanna. Always scheming. Sometimes, I think you're downright wicked.'

'Yes! But it takes one to know one. Jerry told me all kinds of things about you. We should swap notes.' Her fingers gently caress my arm. 'Goodnight, Plum. And remember, no peeking!'

Slipping into the Coffin, I can't help myself. Spurred on by Johanna's warm breath tickling my fancy, I feel under the mattress for the photos and have more than a sneaky peek.

***

This morning, an impenetrable fog envelops us. The world has disappeared. I can barely make out Mickie on the other side of the cockpit. With my eyes an unreliable witness, the ears take over as warning bells ring and fog horns bellow all around us, but I can't find a bearing. Suffice to say we're near San Francisco. Loudest by far are the two fog horns on the Golden Gate Bridge, which blast out distinct notes in a warning pattern; it is a haunting and eerie experience. Sometimes, it's best not to have imagination.

'They sound like the Boom of Doom,' Mickie yells to Arno, who is trying to decipher blips on the radar—the real and present unseen dangers. We're lost in a thick fog thick, a usual event here as it rolls into San Francisco Bay when the cold, wet wind off the sea hits the hot air from the desert. It is a vapor that amplifies sound, making it come from all directions, adding to our disorientation and unease.

'Because we're underpowered,' Arno says to me. 'we've arrived here at the wrong time on two counts.'

'Is one of them you, count?'

'No, the count does not count in my counting.'

'That's a count's way of discounting a count while counting what counts,' Mickie says. 'That's a tongue-twister to twist your tongue.'

'Listen up, you two. Enough with the jokes.' Arno's voice hints at exasperation. 'Tell me this, if you can count so well. If the ebb tide is racing past us at six knots and we are making six knots headway against it, how fast are we moving?'

'We're not moving at all,' Mickie says.

'Precisely! We will have to wait for the tide to change.'

'If time nor tide wait for no man,' I ask. 'Why wait for them?'

'It gives you the time to make some coffee,' Arno suggests, annoyed by the banter. 'We'll sit here, and hope Harry holds up.'

'Ought we to hoot too?' Mickie asks, hearing all the other noises around us. Arno is impressed by his daughter's thinking.

'Brilliant idea! You will make captain one day, *mein Schnucki.*'

'Arrr, shiver me timbers!' Mickie gives me a cheeky grin. 'Appears I'm destined for greatness, Plum bum!'

'Aye, matey, but we've got to make it out of this fog locker first.'

While waiting for slack water, we share the task of blowing blasts from a handheld klaxon. Sure enough, the tide changes, as does the weather. The fog lifts. The horns on the bridge fall silent.

Lucie appears on deck, and we walk to the ship's bow and marvel at the bridge as Arno steers Hoop through it colossal arches. The air is bracing. We snuggle together for warmth.

'Plum. Don't take me wrong, I love Johanna, but when she's around, I never have friends of my own.'

'What do you mean?'

'When we were younger, if anyone called by the house to visit me, she'd never leave us alone. She was always tagging along like a third wheel, but because she's always been so charming and outgoing, they would soon be coming to see her instead of me.'

'Boyfriends, you mean?'

Lucie nods. 'That's why when I overheard her say *our little secret*, alarm bells started ringing. You're my friend, not hers!'

'Oh, Lucie, I had no idea. I'm sorry you feel that way.'

'I know I'm being silly, but I can't help but feel a little jealous in case it's happening with you.'

My mind races, wishing I'd never picked up the pictures.

'I thought you two got on so well.'

'Deep down, we do. Of course, we do, but get this! Hand-me-downs are part of growing up, but sometimes, when Johanna had something, I was looking forward to getting, she'd deliberately tear it or spill a drink over it.'

Being new to sibling rivalry, I'm taken aback.

'Well, I am your friend and won't be stolen.'

'Thanks, Plum,' she says. 'You can be my first mate anytime.'

If only, I think to myself.

San Francisco Bay dwarfs San Diego Bay in size, and Alcatraz, the island fortress prison known for being inescapable until three people did, is impossible to miss. The prison walls loom out of the Bay: grey, cruel, and forbidding. My only notion of life inside is the movie *The Birdman of Alcatraz*. True or false, it conjures up a grim picture of what could have happened if things had gone awry during my escapade with Jerry. I shiver thinking about it. Mark Twain was not exaggerating when he said, "The coldest winter I ever spent was a summer in San Francisco."

Lucie takes over the helm from Johanna, who eagerly follows me down the companionway ladder.

'Better have this back!' I give her the book she put on my bunk earlier, now with photographs slipped between its pages. 'I never finished it.' Snatching it from me, Johanna clutches the book to her chest. As Lucie may be eavesdropping, I emphasize loudly, 'We're not on the same page, and I don't think our tastes match.'

'Not enough pictures in it for you,' she says with a sneer, then hurries off to the privacy of the toilet and bolts the door.

'Johanna's in a funny mood,' says Anna, bumbling about in the galley. 'That film you went to has had a profound effect on her.'

'Well, its message is about being who you want to be.'

'What about the repercussions of doing whatever you want?'

'I thought you were all for self-expression.'

'I'm one for self-improvement, but not spoiling yourself.'

There's a silence in the heads, no pumping and turning of stop cocks, only a slight moan. Then the bolt shoots, and out she steps.

'You look happy,' I say.

'Every picture tells a story.' She breezes out of the cabin, grinning.

Anna regards her with a mix of exasperation and admiration. I sense she's frustrated by her rebelliousness but admires her independent spirit. 'That's Johanna! A handful from day one.'

Limping across the bay, we head for the San Francisco Yacht Club and moor up at a guest berth. The moment we power down, the metallic clanking comes to a halt, and both Arno and I breathe a collective sigh of relief, knowing we've finally made it. After leaving the girls to organize their clothes for a week in port, I follow the skipper to register our arrival with the club committee.

When Count Arno Camaris enters the yacht club he exudes an innate, effortless sense of class. The receptionist falls over himself as he signs in as a reciprocal member.

'This is the finest club west of the Mississippi,' he gushes, pointing out paintings of racing yachts and their illustrious owners. The

Commodore Board is a Who's Who of power. The place oozes class.

'May I point out the club rule that the bar is for men only?'

'What a relief,' Arno says, relaxing on a Chesterfield sofa. 'Bring me a newspaper, a brandy and a fat cigar.'

***

With the family on an evening treat to McDonald's, I leave everything ship-shape and step out to use the club facilities. Rooted in tradition, it couldn't be further from San Francisco's 1970s counterculture scene. It's like comparing hard rock to the barbershop quartet warming up their harmonies at the bar—worlds apart!

Singing in the sweet tones of the Roaring Twenties, the men with dynamic vocal range and perfect control perform a medley of classics, including *Shine on Me* and *Down by the Old Mill Stream*. Their rich harmonies fill the room with warmth and fraternity. The singing is no mere pastiche of striped vests and straw boaters—it is the real deal, conjuring up old money and days spent idling away the hours.

With playful banter and an infectious enjoyment of the genre, they ham it up for me—a new audience. Afterward there's a moment of mortification when I offer to buy them a drink, only to find guest privileges don't go that far. That being the rule, the tenor—a man in his late thirties—orders me one instead. Grateful for a cold beer and an eager ear, I fill him in about the trip. He's most attentive.

'You need a shower,' he says when I finish. 'I can smell you from here. The second club rule is no sweaty jocks in the bar.'

He takes me down to the mahogany-panelled locker room and

points to his locker with its engraved brass escutcheon. 'I inherited it from my daddy.' Throwing me a towel, he points to the sauna cabin. 'You can't come to Frisco and not experience bath culture.'

'Nothing better than a sweat box to relieve tension,' I say, stripping off. He heads to the bathroom, singing the falsetto part of *Give Me Your Hand* while I relax in the bone-warming heat.

It has been a long, hard slog to make it here, but tomorrow, I'm off to catch up with Bob and find out if Nancy is still talking to me. My reverie is interrupted when the tenor comes in, already half pleased to see me. He sheds his wrap and sits down close.

In the cabin's privacy, we grow reckless. While a falsetto voice suggests a pink piccolo, I play an oboe. The piece gets passionate when, by fingering an air hole, the key changes. We crescendo in unison. Our encounter is a brief improvisation. He goes to shower, leaving me wondering if I've infringed another club rule.

***

Today's breakfast is blueberry pancakes, thanks to a stable stove.

'Will you wipe that silly grin off your face?' Johanna says, staring at me. 'You look like the cat that got the cream.'

'I'm on leave. I won't have to stare at your sourpuss face.'

'So Plum, what are you going to do?' Anna asks.

'I'm looking-up an old friend I stayed with when I was last here.'

'What type of friend?' Johanna asks. 'Like your San Juan buddy?'

'No!' I laugh. 'Bob's as straight as an arrow.'

'Does he know you're coming?' Anna asks.

'If he's not home, he'll be at the chess cafe where we used to play.'

'A game of chess!' Arno chimes in. 'I envy you. No responsibilities, only passing pleasures.'

'We have pleasure too,' Anna says, 'We'll be seeing the sights.'

'Take Mickie to the Exploratorium, I worked there once.'

Arno swiftly dismisses the girls' eager requests to go shopping and tells them to find wealthy husbands first.

'That rules me out,' I remark with a chuckle.

Johanna chimes in, 'We're way out of your league.'

Feeling the weight of shipboard fatigue, I get up. 'I'll be off then.'

Lucie's eyes meet mine. 'You will be coming back, won't you?'

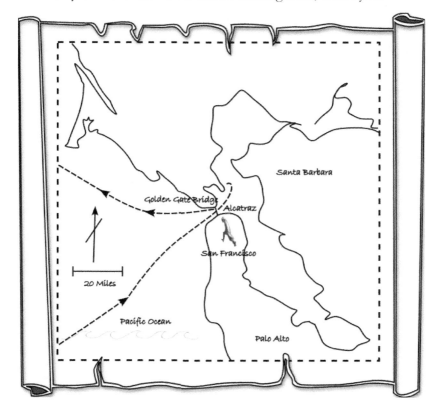

Chapter 14

Game Plan

I take buses from Cavallo Point to Golden Gate Park to find the street where Bob and Nancy live. This is the starting point for my trip down memory lane. Although I have only a rough idea of where I am heading, my limbic brain, which handles getting a drunk home but struggles to fit a key in the lock, kicks in, and I follow its lead.

Soon I'm walking down a familiar street and spot the clapboard house I remember. Pressing the push button, the chimes, designed to calm doorbell nerves, ding dongs inside.

'Might I interest you in double glazing?' I say when a man with a face I recognize opens the door.

'A bad penny always turns up,' Bob says with a smile and ushers me into the kitchen. We met in London in 1969 while working on a fringe theatre show about the Chicago Seven conspiracy trial. Bob handled the publicity photography while I was the lighting technician. William Burroughs played the role of Judge Julius Hoffman. Those were exciting times for us, and even though Bob is older than me, we formed a strong friendship.

'What brings you back to the city?'

'Chance. Fate has brought us together again.'

'Still doing the *I Ching* then?' Bob sniffs.

'Yeah, man, we all need help to understand the unexpected.'

'Well, did serendipity send you here to see me or Nancy?'

'You, of course! But is she still living here?'

'Yup, she'll be back soon,' he says, with a flicker of a smile as though he's discovered my motives. 'Don't expect an easy ride.'

'She took it badly then?'

'What? You dump her to go 'find yourself' and send a postcard marked 'I am here.' What do you reckon, dumb arse?' He pours us both a coffee. 'And to warn you, she's no longer a shrinking violet. She's a fully licensed shrink who'll understand more about your motives than you do.'

'I'll try to avoid any Freudian slips then.'

Sitting in the familiar kitchen, I outline the trip so far and explain how, if things had gone to plan, we'd be in Hawaii, but the winds of change blew us off course, and I ended up here.

'Hold on a sec,' Bob interjects, his eyebrows raised. 'Let's review the situation here, shall we? You've got two sisters on this boat; one thinks you're gay and wants you as a brother, and the other has you all hot and bothered—but she's trouble. It sounds as though you're smack dab in the middle of a sitcom, my friend!'

'That's the crux of it, Bob. I'm all at sea.'

'Well, if you're true to type, you'll avoid emotional commitment and run away. That's your M.O., after all.'

'I've thought of doing that. But I've given the family my word that

I'll go all the way with them to Canada.'

'That's a turn-up for the books. The love rat goes to sea and finds his moral compass!' Bob wriggles uncomfortably in his chair. 'My advice is to steer clear of romance altogether. Invest in a good life jacket, pal. One of them is bound to push you overboard.'

'What if I've met my soulmate?'

Bob looks at me with incredulity. 'Oh, my god. Pass the sick bag. You're not drunk on seawater, are you?'

A key unlocks the back door.

'Look out, here comes trouble,' Bob heads for his darkroom.

Nancy enters clutching a grocery bag close to her chest. With a crackle of paper and rattle of keys, she sets the shopping down.

'Bob!' her New York accent calls out. 'I've got you your haemorrhoid cream.' Then she spots me. 'Well, talk of assholes.'

***

When Bob goes to the bathroom to apply his ointment, I take my medicine and endure an earful from Nancy when my apologies for previous bad behaviour fall on stony ground. She agrees to let me stay, but I suspect Nancy may mete out harsher retribution later.

Ever the diplomat, Bob ushers me out and we head to the Exploratorium where we might bump into Mickie—even Lucie.

'The place is still crazy, and Frank's as mad as ever,' Bob says, lauding its founder, a sibling of Robert Oppenheimer, the brains behind the Manhattan Project.

'Must be tough having the father of the atomic bomb as your

brother,' I say, remembering the connection.

'Scientists are inquisitive people. They're morally agnostic and only interested in advancing knowledge.'

We enter the north wing of the Palace of Fine Arts, a monumental building from a bygone era, which now houses Frank's brainchild— his space to foster wonder, critical thinking, and curiosity in people of all ages. As befits a man on a mission, he's here. We head over to a group of students enthralled by his passion and enthusiasm.

'The understanding of the universe is governed by three fundamental laws that describe the relationship between heat, work, and energy,' he explains before breaking them down further. 'To remember thermodynamics easily, keep in mind these three principles: firstly, you can't win; secondly, you can't break even; and thirdly, you can't quit the game.'

'That about sums up your situation,' Bob says, acknowledging Frank, who waves his walking cane at us before heading off at breakneck speed with a crowd trailing in his wake.

'Follow me,' says Bob. 'I will show you one of the new exhibits that takes photography to another level.'

'What do you think of that?' he says, leading me to a room where a three-dimensional illusion of a detached head floats in space like a sci-fi movie. 'It's a hologram. The first ever seen in public.'

Trying to work out where the magic is coming from, my eyes widen in surprise. It's a glimpse into a future, where anything is possible. 'Crazy, man, that's far out!'

'What great feedback! Thanks for your piercing and incisive critique—definitely one for the history books.'

***

It feels great to be off the boat, but spending time with old friends has drawbacks. They know your history and can burst your bubble. During breakfast, Nancy analyses the detailed account of the adventures I shared with her over supper, accompanied by too much wine. I blurted out more than was wise, including the sauna incident.

'So, you've reinvented yourself into some gay Billy Budd?' she says with a hint of sarcasm before adding. 'Y'know what? One day you'll figure out who you really are.'

'I can't understand why they all believe it.'

'You aren't that insightful, are you?' she continues, limbering up. 'First, you lived with an openly gay man in Puerto Rico. Second, you worked in the theatre. The clues are all there. Perhaps that's why you ran out on me—you're gay and refuse to admit it.'

'Hmmm, interesting. The parents accept it too.'

'Oh, for goodness' sake! They're of the generation that knows actors are, at best, sexually ambivalent, and the artistic temperament is a social exception to the norm. In their eyes, you're one less thing to worry about.'

'The skipper describes me as harmless!'

'He's right! There's something about you that's damaged, weak, soft-centred—probably why I fell for you back then.'

Saved by the bell, Bob waves us away and takes a phone call.

216

Not finished with me, Nancy picks up her keys. 'Come Mariner Mick! Show me this Rhine maiden you drooled about last night.'

'Did I?' I say, unaware I had admitted to anything.

'Yes, Lucie. A capable young woman who's captured your heart, and you can't wait to ruin her in your careless arms. And you don't tell her you're straight in order to keep up a smokescreen and avoid her rejection.'

'Bloody hell, Nancy. How much do you charge?'

'More than you can afford. Now let's go.' Laughing, she drags me out to the car.

Nancy is driving a stylish, metallic-silver Karmann Ghia coupe. Although I'm alarmed at the high speeds we're reaching—speeds I've forgotten existed—what's even more concerning is that as I catch sight of the marina—*Hoop* has disappeared.

The concierge hands me a note left at reception, and my heart jumps into my mouth. '*Plum, Papa's moved us to a maintenance dock up the creek to fix the engine, as the club rules don't allow repairs on-site. See you back here on Friday. Love, Lucie XXX.*'

Nancy examines the handwriting. 'More mature than I thought.' She then sneaks a peek through the glass doors. 'This is a classy joint.'

'Let me show you around.' I reach for the door handle.

'Excuse me, sir,' the concierge says firmly. 'Access is for members only. While your employer, his Excellency the Count, has privileges, without him, crew members are not to be admitted.'

'That put you in your place,' Nancy sniggers. 'The elder sister's right. You're punching above your weight.'

'That's not a nice thing to say,' I reply. 'I am going to punch the porter in the nose.' Nancy leads me away.

'That's not kind either. You take risks with other people without considering the consequences,' she says, popping into analyst mode. 'Impulsive behaviour is a syndrome. Simply because you can do something doesn't mean you should.' Sensing me getting all defensive, she changes tack. 'Let's head up to the Fireman's Hose. You might spot up boat, and you can wave to your love interest.'

I sigh, aware of the sarcasm in her words. It's a gentle reminder that Nancy hasn't forgiven me for my misadventure. 'What, Coitus Tower. Where we first kissed, or have you forgotten?'

'Oh no!' Nancy laughs—the sound is derisive. 'Our little fling was a one-time thing. I'm not interested in a repeat performance. You may not have found yourself, but I have!'

Legend has it that Lillie Hitchcock Coit, a wealthy benefactor, erected the Art Déco tower in the 1920s to resemble a firehose nozzle because of her close affinity with the city's firefighters. It stands tall atop Telegraph Hill, with a panoramic view of Nob Hill, Russian Hill, Twin Peaks, the Financial District, the Ferry Building, the bay, and all its bridges and islands. But there's no sign of *Hoop*.

Nancy points to the parking space where we had made out. 'Remember how reckless we were up here?'

'We had fun,' I say getting in the car. 'Why don't we park up?'

Nancy's haughty sniff says it all as she slips the clutch. 'Steady, tiger. It's not ethical to sleep with clients, even pro bono ones.'

In the morning, Bob and I head to a coffee shop for a nostalgic chess game. It still has the club atmosphere I used to love when we hung out here and evokes a sense of comfort and familiarity.

He wants to show me his black-and-white prints of anti-Vietnam War protests now hanging on the wall. They are brutally honest.

'These guys are all wounded veterans,' he says, putting names to faces. 'It's shocking that war veterans suffering from debilitating injuries are neglected and left without government support. This moral outrage occurs right under our noses while the public seemingly turns a blind eye. I am committed to documenting it.'

Male-dominated and competitive, the atmosphere is intense, with little socializing. Finding an empty table, we sit beside players wreathed in a haze of cigarette smoke, creating an intellectually stimulating yet funky atmosphere. Already I'm intimidated, as I've never won a game against Bob.

'Now, let's have some maturity in your play,' Bob whispers, his voice barely audible in the hushed atmosphere of the room. 'Don't revert to making weak moves out of frustration.'

Following the traditional method of deciding who goes first, I set out eight white pawns, my palms already clammy.

'Out of interest,' he says as I ponder my first move, 'what is your plan now that you've given up on your theatre career? The one area where you had a bankable talent.'

'I'm trying to figure that out.' I reply with King Pawn Opening.

'That's what this trip is all about.'

'Bullshit!' He snorts responding to the open game 'You're drifting about, rudderless.' I bring out my knight. 'You were 'finding yourself' the last time you passed through.' he says, making a similar move.

I move a bishop ready to castle. 'I've come to report on progress.'

Bob moves his bishop. 'You mistake me for someone who gives a damn. But as you're looking for a guru to guide your aimless mind, I'll give it to you straight. In short, you are a loser.'

'That's a bit harsh.' I bridle, capturing his pawn in defiance.

He pounces on my blunder by threatening my knight.

As it's pinned to my king he whisks it away on his next move.

'Hey, you can't do that,' I complain. 'I need it for my plan.'

'That's not how it works.' He places my captured piece on the side. 'I don't see a plan in your game, let alone your life.'

'I'm following my path, waiting for a sign,' I move a pawn.

'Well then, until you find this great calling, you'd better do your best by other people and help get this family back to Canada.'

'Why are you being so hard on me?' I say trying to figure his move

'Why should I go easy on you?'

'Or I on you!' I make a move to turn the tide and win me the game.

'You can't do that,' he points out with irritation. 'You're in check.'

'You could have told me,' I complain.

'Not my job. Work these things out for yourself.'

Searching the board for a way out, I'm astonished at how fast this game has fallen apart. Sensing my discomfort, Bob riles me. 'You're in the shit because of past moves; decisions have consequences.'

'Why are you so mean?' I sigh realizing the game's up.

'Wow, did somebody steal your rudder? It's because I'm crazy about my stepsister Nancy, dumb-ass,' he whispers while wiping out my queen with one of his stallions. I slump back in disbelief.

'Bob, why didn't you tell me?'

'What's the point. I'm the brother she never had. End of!' For a moment, he's sliding down an ice sheet, trying to hold on. Then he snaps back to the game. 'Oh! For god's sake, let's finish this in silence until it's time for me to say checkmate.'

We play on to the tick of chess clocks. Then he traps my king.

'Congratulations Bob, you've always been a winner.'

'Zip it, Limey! You're so full of shit you make a sewer smell sweet.'

***

The next day, we walk from Haight Ashbury to Golden Gate Park for a stroll around Stow Lake before I catch a bus to the yacht club.

'I might have been harsh on you yesterday,' Bob says.

'No, you weren't,' I say. 'Your revelation about Nancy blows me away. How long have you loved her?'

'A year ago, she went to work. Her lingering scent took me by surprise, and I knew what the feeling in the pit of my stomach meant.'

'What's the chance of you getting together?'

'What, stepsiblings making out? Not a chance! Even if Nancy felt the same. Too many deal-breakers. But we bought the house together so I've the next best thing. We're joined everywhere but at the hip.'

'But doesn't it break your heart, seeing her every day?'

'Luckily, I'm not chained to an idiot's dick as you are. I count my blessings and bury myself in my work.'

'I'm sorry I came back and upset the apple cart.'

'Don't be! And you didn't. Nancy got a bit of revenge. I thrashed you at chess. All's good under the hood.'

We sit staring at the lake's Chinese pavilion.

'Leave me here, Bob. I'll find my way back.'

'No can do, bud.' He pulls me up. 'I promised Nancy to see you out to sea. You've got a date with destiny.'

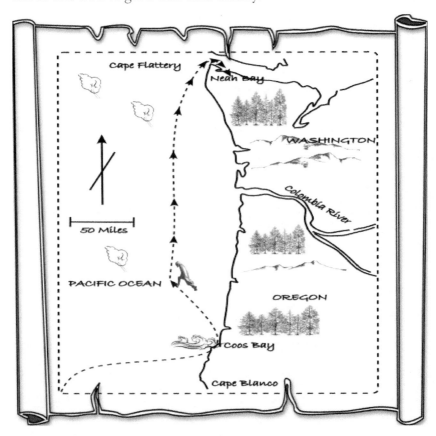

Chapter 15

Venus Rising

Bob's criticism is a much-needed push, and I step back on board, determined to prove myself. My return is prompt as Arno, relieved he got the engine repaired, is itching to be underway. Together, we listen to the sound of well-oiled machines. But he's not happy.

'I have had my fair share of run-ins with boat mechanics. This lot milked me for every dime. It's enough to make you throw in the anchor. But what can you do? I had to bite the bullet and pay the price—*Hoop* has to make it home. My future depends on it.'

So saying, he sends me down the deck to cast off and begin our last leg home. When I return to the cockpit, Lucie comes out of the saloon. However, she doesn't acknowledge my presence and looks away. I'm baffled. I've never seen a shoulder so cold. Something happened while was away?

Before I can find out, the ebb tide propels us out from under the Golden Gate Bridge like a bullet from a gun. We end up in a section of choppy water known as the *cabbage patch*. From there, we navigate the shipping channels and then head northwest toward windswept seas. Leaving Arno putting Dick and Harry through their paces, I go below and throw my gear into the Coffin.

In the galley, Anna and Mickie are packing away provisions. 'Sorry about your bed being in a mess,' Anna says. 'Lucie was making it but apparently got distracted. We were going to move you into Jerry's old cabin, but the girls have had one of their usual rows over nothing. It's sisters being sisters. They may bicker and squabble, but deep down, they love each other. I've put them into separate cabins until it blows over.'

Giving Mickie a 'what's going on?' look, she returns a 'no idea' shrug, being more interested in watching where her mum is stowing our new survival rations. These include Mug-o-Lunch Mac and Cheese, Space Food Sticks, chocolate-covered Graham Crackers and other delights that Anna, expecting bad weather, will provide as snacks when it's too rough to cook. 'The days of civilized meals may be over,' she notes.

'Wanna be amazed?' Mickie says, riffling a crisp new pack of cards.

'Did you buy them in a magic shop?' I ask.

'Slam dunk to me!' she declares in triumph. 'You said magic didn't exist. How come I can find a shop that sells it?'

Outsmarted by the little tyke, I raise an imaginary hat in respect and head off to find Johanna, hoping she can shed light on why Lucie's ignoring me.

Knocking on her door, she invites me in as if she knew I was coming. She's on the bed, flipping through Cosmopolitan magazine.

'What's wrong with Lucie? She blanked me like I don't exist.'

'Haven't a clue, Plum. Lucie can be fickle,' Johanna fakes a yawn.

'One day, you're gold; the next, you're poop. It's time to move on.'

'What's gone on? Anna says you two have had a row.'

Johanna tosses the magazine aside. 'The crush she had on you is over. I've seen to that!' Johanna examines her fingernails. 'I told you, Plum, Lucie hates deception and is as stubborn as a mule. You can't change her mind now.' She's a triumphant glint in her eyes. 'Close the door as you leave. I'm sure you have duties to perform.'

***

Today, we begin a five-day race to cover the 725 nautical miles to Neah Bay, our last anchorage before the final sprint up the Strait of Juan de Fuca to Vancouver. Arno has the bit between his teeth and intends to push hard.

'We must use this window of good weather to press on,' he calls up from the chart table after listening to fishermen talking on the radio. He believes that if they are at sea, *Hoop* can be, too. However, progress is more about moving up and down than moving forward.

The way Arno set the watch schedule means I haven't seen Lucie for days. She's up when I'm asleep, and vice versa. Even in a boat this size she is elusive. I hear her, but when I turn around, she's gone. Much like with the *Klabautermann*, it's best if I don't bump into her.

Per our orders, we sail closer to the shore to avoid the strong current and keep our speed at seven knots. We're on and off the watch like clockwork dolls, which is tiring. It can feel lonely out here, especially at night when the rotating radar screen is the only companion. With Lucie ignoring me and Johanna being smug, I feel nostalgic for the better times, and melancholy creeps over me.

Someway ahead I spot a ship with a bright, stern light. It glows more brilliantly by the minute as we gain on it. Then, as my friendship with Lucie has done, the light goes out. Nothing shows on the radar. Could the vessel have sunk, or is my mind playing tricks? Then, it strikes me that we are following nothing. It was Venus rising before disappearing behind a cloud. The song "Venus in Blue Jeans" pops into my head. It's about the girl who stole my heart, the Cinderella I adore. Regardless of Lucie's lack of a ponytail, I find comfort in Hank Williams' "Lovesick Blues", where man's follies run wild.

Singing in my head, I try to figure out how Johanna ruined it. What's this deception she talks about? While trying to puzzle it out, Mickie hands me one of Anna's helmsman's treats, so the problem is consigned to the bilge to slosh around unsolved.

'Plum, you seem glum.'

'All the magic's gone, Mickie,' I say, forcing a smile.

'Thought you said it doesn't exist.'

'I mean the magic that's more than a sleight of hand.'

'You mean a fantasy when we see things that aren't real?'

'Yes,' I say. 'A flight of fancy. One puff and it's gone.'

A lash of sea spray crashes over the cockpit. With a cold splash of reality, I come to my senses as a rolling swell makes *Hoop* gripe and a pig to steer.

***

The weather is unusual here, with cloud formations unlike any I've seen before. As we travel past rocky capes and headlands, vortices form in the stratocumulus layer. Each one a miniature twister, they twirl and whirl with frenetic energy as if alive.

We round Cape Arago after a complete cycle of watch-taking. This jagged point of land juts out into the sea about a mile from the general trend of the coast, and its lighthouse blinks on and off through the gloom, warning of offshore reefs. When a thunderstorm moves in, our situation becomes fraught. Regular lightning flashes illuminate an angry sky as a change in the wind whips up the sea, bringing heavy rain that crashes over the deck. I am enduring a torrid spell at the helm, hunkered down in foul-weather gear, ducking each time thunder cracks overhead. When my shift ends, the storm clouds disperse, revealing the first stars twinkling in the sky. Arno is due to replace me soon, and the worst of the weather has passed.

The North Pacific is a beast with a reputation as wild as the bears that roam the coast. Arno is still figuring out the risks in navigating this passage, so we slip further out to sea at night to avoid crashing into the multitude of crab pots that litter the waters. We're facing rough waves, causing *Hoop* to sway and stumble. At the helm, I predict their size and direction, hoping to avoid breaking crests.

Dawn comes, raw and grey, with a sea mist, and I must take a second look to make sure my eyes aren't deceiving me. Appearing out of the haze, a massive fleet of boats charges towards us like wild beasts. Wave after wave storm past in pursuit of sockeye salmon. The trawlers sluice the water at speed and bully us with their wake. Pots and pans clatter in the galley, and hearing Anna come close to cursing, I yell an apology about events outside my control.

Midway through my shift, as conditions settle, Mickie goes on aloft to spreadeagle up the weather-side ratlines on the lookout. Hazards come in all shapes and sizes, ranging from fishing gear to half-submerged logs carried downstream and entangled in clusters of kelp. From her vantage point, Mickie's keen eye is right for the job.

'Plum Bum,' she shouts. 'There's a floater ahead.'

'What is it, rigging monkey? Animal, vegetable or mineral?'

'Well, it's not an iceberg,' she wisecracks back, stretching for a better view and putting a hand up against the glare.

Hoop lurches hard as a nasty wave hits us side-on. Mickie screams and cartwheels out of the rigging, her hands grasping for something to grab. She bounces off the cabin roof and crumples onto the deck.

'Man overboard!' I yell as I struggle to navigate toward a smoother patch of water. Arno comes up to the cockpit, looking worried, and scans the water. I point towards a crushed bundle in the scuppers. He steps onto the deck, about to scoop Mickie up. 'Don't move her!' Lucie shouts, bounding up beside him. 'She might be hurt!'

The boat rocks as the scene unfolds; it's as if I'm viewing the world through a camera lens, each detail heightened and magnified. Everyone's frozen in time, waiting to find out what cruel trick fate has played on us. Anna's expression bears the weight of a mother's anguish. Johanna bites her lip. The silence is deafening. Each second is an eternity as Lucie assesses the damage.

A sense of relief washes over us as Mickie regains consciousness. Lucie checks if there is any other damage besides having the wind knocked out of her. Calm and controlled, she gets Mickie to wiggle her fingers and toes. She cries out in agony, trying to lift her left arm. We all realize that something is wrong.

'Stabilize the shoulder,' Anna says, opening her medical bag of tricks and passing over some bandages.

'Bind it where you find it,' Lucie instructs herself on autopilot, strapping the arm against Mickie's chest.

'Lucie took a First-Aid course,' Johanna exclaims, her voice filled with shock and irony. 'It's unbelievable that a crisis would strike when we're this close to home.'

Arno gathers Mickie in his arms, shouting, 'Make way! Make way!' as he carries her to the cockpit and lays her on the cushioned seat. Anna examines her eyes for concussion. 'We've got to get her to a hospital,' she says emphatically.

Arno goes on the radio. A fisherman advises that, as the injury isn't critical and we're close to the shore, we shouldn't call for an emergency evacuation at sea but head to port.

Lucie takes over the helm from me as we make for Coos Bay, the nearest harbour with a medical facility that routinely manages maritime injuries. It is only an hour's sailing past Cape Arago.

'Well done. You handled that crisis with a cool head.'

'Don't you patronize me,' she replies, slapping the compliment down. 'What were you doing letting Mickie climb the rigging in these conditions? I thought you were an experienced deckhand.' She guns the engine to full throttle. 'Go and see if you've damaged the boat. And stay up front on lookout duty.'

With a shrug of the shoulders, I go and sit on the naughty step.

***

Being five miles out to sea, we make top speed towards the river estuary at Coos Bay and the hardscrabble harbour beyond. Here, Arno has to either wait three hours for the tide to change or take a wild ride over the sandbar at the river mouth. The count decides to run the bar, as Mickie may have suffered internal injuries. However, we face a challenge where the ebb tide flows against an incoming sea, creating monstrous breaking waves we'll have to navigate.

Beefing up Lucie on the helm, Arno orders me to tie myself on and report back on the positions of the marker buoys as they dip up and down in the whirlpool. With Mickie strapped down and Anna and Johanna told to stay below and hold on tight, we charge into the fray. Arno shows his skill by matching our speed to that of the waves to avoid surfing and broaching. Under his sure hand, we ride on the back of one swell after another, always just ahead of the one behind. After minutes of back-breaking work at the wheel and a bone-shaking shudder as we touch the bottom, *Hoop* yaws, slews, and wallows her way into the estuary's calmer waters and our rollercoaster comes to the end of the ride.

The sheltering shoreline is a sand spit covered with high dunes, topped by rugged, windswept trees. The river curves inland, and low-pitched houses nestle among rolling hills. Johanna and I lay out the dock lines as we approach a sturdy wooden jetty and boardwalk. A small crowd has gathered, and an ambulance is waiting. After local fishermen help me tie up, Arno receives applause as he walks down the gangway with Mickie in his arms. It is a mark of respect for a captain crossing the bar for an injured crew member.

Watching them head off to the medical facility with Mickie is a relief. The drama is over. A crisis averted, but with Johanna left behind, a melodrama is about to begin.

'You can take me out for a drink,' she says. 'We need to talk.'

Arno instructed me to inform the harbourmaster of our arrival, and now I find myself in his office, getting a sense of our location. The walls are hung with old, framed photographs of the resilient fishermen, loggers, and sawmill workers who built this place. Their expressions reflect a determination and stubborn defiance—pure pioneer spirit—men who are miserable until they're paid and only happy once they're broke again.

'Going native?' Johanna says, seeing I haven't shaved. She's taken great pains over her appearance and is wearing the prairie dress she wore to the party.

'Here I need a rugged outdoorsy look,' I say, ruffling my hair. 'I've seen where we're going and it ain't pretty.'

***

Dive bars such as this attract clientele who live for the moment as renegades and choose to get drunk in fistfight territory; where John Wayne etiquette allows the use of chairs as weapons, but knives are off-limits—it's that type of place. Five tattooed fishermen sit at the bar, bum cracks in view.

Johanna glares at me and goes, 'You must be joking?' I mean, seriously? As though today hasn't been enough of a wild ride.'

'Believe me, the only other joint is worse. It's for loggers, and the dudes who helped us tie up pointed me to this spot. If we want a drink, it's got to be The Drunken Doozy.'

Inside, a Jimmy Buffett song is playing. Lounging by the pool table, a hustler chalks his cue. He's the type who will let you win a few games and then double down, make a few 'lucky shots', and threaten to break your legs unless you pay up quick.

In case an English accent provokes a reaction in one of these fellas whose way of life is cigarettes, cheap beer, and outbursts of violence, I play dumb, keep my mouth shut, and point to a booth by the door.

'All right, what's your poison? We've got dreams on the rocks, illusions with a splash, and a shot of reality,' the waitress asks.

I sign language 'beer' to Johanna; she signs 'wanker' back.

'Two beers, please. My friend has lost his tongue.'

'Don't worry, honey. Most guys here can't string a sentence together.'

'Yes, but a tongue has other purposes,' Johanna says.

The waitress, a 'call 'em like she sees em' type working a dead-end job, smiles. 'Whatever floats your boat's fine by me.'

When she goes, I lean in, whispering, 'You're outrageous! You've no shame?'

Johanna throws back her head, laughing. 'Not anymore.'

Out of nowhere, the saloon door swings open Wild West style. Reeking of sawdust, a hammered lumberjack stumbles my way, yelling, 'Hey, fish lips. Bet no-one puckers up to a gob that tastes of fish guts!'

Johanna's hand clamps over her mouth, her bottled breath about to burst out laughing. Regardless of the lumberjack tossing out an age-old challenge to fight, I chicken out and resort to a pantomime of faking deafness. Baffled, he doubles down, but it's like tossing pebbles at a tank. He stumbles out to a chorus of barfly laughter.

'Jerry would have killed the weasel-faced little twerp.'

'Well, it's a good thing he ran away from you before we got here,' I counter, turning the jab around.

Before she can answer, the waitress returns. 'Sorry about that little disruption, folks. That wrangling lumberjack is a Friday night regular. You saved us a broken bar stool. Here's drinks on the house.'

'Brains beats brawn every round,' I reply, chug-a-luggin'.

'Well, your boyfriend's not so dumb after all.'

Johanna leans across to wipe a foam moustache off my lip. I recoil at her touch.

'I get it, Plum, I do. You can't stand the sight of me, but hey, it's my way of protecting Lucie.'

'Alright, convince me! What's the deal with Lucie needing you as her protector?'

Johanna sucks the beer spume off her finger. 'It's the usual drill. *Hoop* makes a pit stop, and guys come looking for easy pickings. Papa invites anyone aboard, hoping for a son-in-law, while Mama's running on fumes, tries to manage the chaos. We're a travelling circus and *Hoop*'s the big tent.'

'Seriously, Johanna. I've watched you turn the current on and demand attention.'

'Yes. But with Lucie, it's different.'

'Why?'

'She's not gone all the way yet.'

'What, she's a virgin?'

'Yes. I've always protected Lucie from men. She hates me for it, but isn't it what a big sis is supposed to do?'

Taking a sip, I gaze into the glass. Johanna's flipped the switch— but it doesn't stack up. I throw in a curveball. 'She told me you ruined the clothes she's about to have as hand-me-downs. What's that all about?' I hit a nerve.

Taken aback, Johanna's eyes widen as her mouth opens in surprise. 'Lucie said that?'

'Yes, it pisses her off. Are you worried that she might outshine you?' Rumbled, there's fury in Johanna's eyes, but I don't let up. 'Why are you so controlling?'

Johanna lowers her voice, sighs, and gives me that 'you won't believe what I've been through' look.

'In Canada, the age of consent is fourteen. A guy at school forced himself on me and told all his buddies I'd let him. I didn't want that to happen to Lucie.'

'But why protect her now? She's nearly twenty.' I snap, annoyed by her emotional manipulation.

Johanna toys with her beer. 'Habit, I suppose.'

I don't buy it. 'She hinted about a boyfriend.'

'He's a religious nut and harmless. They're perfectly suited. Both as pure as the driven snow.'

Rising from the table while reaching into my pocket for a tip, I place it under my empty glass before looking at her steadily. 'I felt a spark with Lucie. A spark like no other.'

'Yes, I noticed, and she was falling for you. But I've ruined it for you. You'll have to get over Lucie. You're not good enough for her.'

I take a deep breath, trying to maintain my composure. 'Can you tell me exactly how you ruined it?' I ask, my voice strained as I struggle to control my anger.

Johanna smirks, clearly enjoying my discomfort. 'Simple,' she says, her tone mocking. 'She thinks you've fallen for me.'

*****

It's dark when we return to *Hoop*. The others are back. Lucie's tone is laced with sarcasm as we climb on board.

'Been out having fun while we've been worried sick about Mickie?'

Ignoring her, I head down to the saloon.

'How's the patient?'

A sigh of relief washes over Arno's face as he swivels from the chart table. 'The bad news is that Mickie won't be attempting any more acrobatics. The good news is that she only fractured her radius. Nothing to stop us from continuing our journey.'

'We went to urgent care,' Anna adds, a weight lifted off her shoulders. 'They put on a temporary cast to stabilize the arm. We will find an orthopaedic surgeon in Vancouver. The swelling's too much to set permanently now.'

Mickie exposes the slab of plaster under a sling.

'Can I be the first to sign it?' I ask.

'Sure,' she says, as I scribble, *No more cards up your sleeve for a while!* 'And Plum, to answer your question, it was a deadhead.'

'Well, we missed it,' I laugh, amazed at her resilience.

'What's a deadhead?' Anna asks, intrigued.

'It's a half-sunken log bobbing out of sight,' Mickie explains.

'And before this trip,' I add, 'I thought it was a Grateful Dead fan.'

***

The sound of fishermen bustling up and down the pier in the early hours wakes me. Then a rumble of boat engines sees Arno on deck, listening to the muted hum of crews moving about with practiced efficiency. With the count just as eager to be underway, he starts the engines. I make coffee and break out the glazed doughnuts Anna bought yesterday. When the rhythmic clinking of anchor chains against metal signals the beginning of another salmon hunt, Arno shouts his order, 'First mate! Let go of the bow line!' Keeping our distance, we follow the fleet out to sea.

Once we're into open water, I take the helm while Arno plots a course. If all goes according to plan, the next sight of land should be Cape Flattery in two days, where we will leave the ocean and head inland down the Strait of Juan de Fuca, the body of water that separates the Olympic Peninsula from Vancouver Island.

Dick and Harry thrum beneath the deck, cutting through the morning mist, pushing *Hoop* forward to her journey's end. My three-thousand-mile trip aboard blurs into a dream that once promised boundless horizons but now confronts the limits of time and tide. I stand at the helm, contemplating the closing chapter, each mile marking the relentless advance to an uncertain future.

Hoop is soon far enough off the coast that only the snow-covered peaks of the Cascade Range loom in the distance. Otherwise, the day is as dull as a Sunday sermon. Mickie and I come up with tongue-twisters to alleviate the boredom.

'Slick Mick, thick as a brick, flicks a stick at Dick.'

'Sicky Mickie, err…' I say, faltering in search of rhymes.

'Land Ho!' she shouts me down as I blurt out, 'Sicky Mickie, picky cardy tricky.' In an instant, Arno appears with binoculars trained at the grey lump on the horizon.

'There is Cape Flattery—the northwesternmost point of the contiguous United States.'

Hoop cleaves through the Pacific brine, and details appear in the towering precipice rising from the sea. A lighthouse sits atop a bluff.

Buffeted by the elements, it's a resolute sentinel guiding us home. Down below, the ocean crashes against the craggy cliffs, where long-lost logs are scattered among the rocks. Above us, seabirds soar on the updrafts and cry out into the wind-torn sky.

'Cape Flattery's battery is the gulls' squawky chattery,' Mickie says, going below. 'I'm hungry.'

***

Turning to starboard, our compass heading points east. We've stopped moving north and are sailing towards Neah Bay, the anchorage for our last night in US waters, which lies within the ancestral territory of the Makah tribe.

With a hopeful gaze toward smoother water, Anna quips, 'More coffee in your mug and less on your shirt from now on, Plum.'

Touched by her thoughtfulness until the very last moment, I accept her warm brew as a shield against the chilly wind. We pass by jagged rock formations that serve as homes to grunting puffins and diving seabirds. After a few hours of motoring, we turn into a broad horseshoe bay. Here, the waves and swells of the ocean die down. Above a sloping sandy beach is a fishing village of rough-board houses made from the towering spruce forest stretching to infinity.

With ample space to swing with the tide, we drop anchor and let out an extended chain length. Knowing it's the last time I'll hear it crunch and grind in the bow roller, I gaze down into the clear water as *Hoop*'s hook hurries to the bottom.

Like milk spilled over a table, a layer of mist seeps into the bay. In the gloaming, I hear a rhythmic chant coming ever closer. Then, breaking through the brume, a cedar-log war canoe with a carved eagle prow slips past. Aboard, eight members of the Makah tribe drive their painted paddles through the water and disappear into the fog. It's a fleeting glimpse into legend. An echo of the past.

***

This afternoon, doing shipboard chores, I get an idea for Mickie's last elocution lesson. Despite her being irritable and touchy, I'll miss our one-to-ones. Anna hinted she's started her periods, which might explain it. But today, she's as bright as a button. Our lesson is off to a flying start.

'Let's name it an Electrocution Lesson,' she suggests with her familiar mischievous smile. 'Then I can say something shocking.'

'It's not cool to laugh at your own jokes.'

'How do you cope every morning when you have to look in the mirror?'

'The most shocking thing I had to recite when I was young was a song my mother taught me. It's called the *Hearse Song*. Want to learn it too?'

'As long as I don't die laughing.'

'Well, it goes like this:
You may laugh as the hearse rolls by
But you may be the next to die
They wrap you up in a long white sheet
And drop you down about ten feet

All goes well for about a week

Until the coffin begins to leak

Worms come in, and worms go out

They come in thin and go out stout.'

'Nice try, Plum! But you need lessons to improve your memory. You forgot the verse that goes...

They eat your eyes,

They eat your nose.

And eat the jelly between your toes.'

I glance at Anna, who's in the galley cooking supper. 'Missus C, my work here is done.'

Anna nods her head and passes me a cup. 'Here, Plum, have some coffee with a nice tot of rum.'

'Thanks, I'll take this on deck as the sun go down.'

Up here, all is quiet, and I sip my coffee while watching the light fade on the water. As the last glimmer of sunlight silhouettes the conical spires of the conifers around the bay, the wail of a loon punctuates the eerie calm. Its long, mournful call evokes the solitude of the place, but then a haunting response echoes back over the water, reassuring its mate all is well.

Involuntarily, I cry out, too, but no reply comes back. I feel as alone as an abandoned child. That waterbird's plaintive question, 'I'm here; where are you?' unravels the layers of self-assurance I've built over the years, leaving me facing the stark reality that you can't paper over cracks forever.

'Dinner's ready,' Johanna calls up from the galley.

'I'll pass. I'm not hungry.'

'Please yourself. We're having sausage and sauerkraut, but we've run out of mustard.'

***

Weary, I lie in my bunk, spellbound by the rhythmic cadence of water on the hull as it composes maritime poetry, whispering cryptic tales in murmurs and sighs. Slipping into slumber, I dream of seeing the *Klabautermann* and foundering on the rocks.

A sudden jolt of terror wakes me to confront that I will disembark alone onto a strange shore tomorrow. The uncertainty gnaws in the pit of my stomach. Out of sorts, I lie awake until dawn's cold, grey light seeps through the porthole.

Glad to be out of bed, I shuffle deckward to check if the anchor has dragged its mooring overnight. I bump into Lucie standing on the foredeck, wrapped in a blanket, staring at the distant silhouette of her rocky mountain home. Morning musings and maritime routines collide, leaving us alone for the first time since Frisco.

'Penny for your thoughts?' Her hair is tied back but a hint of morning breeze tousles the strands she missed.

'I'm not in the habit of selling them,' she says, closing down the exchange. Her cobalt eyes flash a warning sign as she walks away.

I sidestep, blocking her. 'What's up, Lucie? You've been ignoring me for days. It's as though I don't exist.'

'What's my business to do with a dirty little deckhand?'

'Come on, that's a bit harsh. We were getting along so well. Then, suddenly, you're the Ice-Maiden.'

'You betrayed me, simple as that.'

'Betrayed you! How?'

'The photograph. How could you? After all we'd talked about.'

'What photograph?'

'The Polaroid of Johanna.'

I stand stunned. The revelation stops me cold. It is the last thing I expected. I don't have them anymore, and Lucie mentions one. Why? Before I answer, she is at me.

'All this about being gay.' I sense her anger rising. 'You're not queer, but a pervert. Now, out of my way!'

'Lucie! Let me explain. You've got this all wrong.'

'I doubt an explanation will make a difference,' she replies with cold disdain. 'I found a picture of my sister under your mattress. That's wrong on so many levels I don't know where to start.'

My mind is racing, trying to keep up. Maybe I left out a photograph when I gave the book to Johanna before going ashore.

Fighting a rising panic that she found a picture, I blurt, 'Lucie, you've got it all wrong. Let me lay it out for you. You owe me that.'

'You've got a minute. I'm getting cold.'

Steady now, I think to myself. *This is your one shot. After all, this is about a picture I didn't even take. Okay, take a deep breath, focus, let the truth unfold, and make every word count.* 'Remember when we were leaving the party, and I went to fetch Johanna? She was in bed with that photographer.'

'Well, that's wrong for a start,' Lucie interrupts. 'She told me it was someone much more famous.'

'Lucie, I swear it was the photographer. I saw him. I was there.'

'So?' she shrugs as if my words hold no weight.

'Well, compromising Polaroids of Johanna were lying around, so I scooped them up to protect her,' I explain, my words hanging in the air. The look on Lucie's face leaves me hanging like Wily Coyote.

'Plum. What are you talking about? The one I found in your bunk isn't compromising at all. Johanna looks gorgeous. You took it before we had our hair cut. It has nothing to do with the party.' Her arms fly up in frustration, and the blanket wrapped around her falls to the deck. 'I don't know why I'm even listening to you.'

'Oh, my god,' I gasp as the penny drops—this is ridiculous. 'When did you find it?'

'When you were away, I wanted your bed to be fresh when you returned. As though I should care.' Lucie tries to push by. 'I don't see where this is getting us.'

Realizing her mind's made up, I try a different tack.

'You know all this stuff about me being gay?'

'Yes, but what's that got to do with it?'

'Have I ever told you I'm gay? No! It was a tale Jerry spun to sideline me, and somehow, you all got caught up in it.'

'Now it's our fault?' Her voice is defensive and volatile.

'No, it's not about blame. It was a role I played. A façade because I didn't want…'

'Didn't want what?'

Looking away, I mutter, embarrassed. 'Any complications.'

Lucie raises an eyebrow. 'What do you mean?

'Getting involved with anyone. I was dealing with personal stuff, and the last thing I wanted was emotional entanglements.'

'Emotional entanglements?' She asks, intrigued.

I met her gaze. 'I needed breathing room to sort myself out.'

'Sort yourself out, why?'

'I run away from commitment. I wanted to stay detached so played along with the gay story to keep things simple.'

'What! You thought one of us might fall for you? As if!' Lucie pauses momentarily. 'It still doesn't explain why you have a photograph of my sister under your bed. And you can't understand why I'm upset? Are all men this stupid, or are you a special case?'

I take a deep breath, hesitant to say it, but it's my last resort. 'Because that's where Johanna put it.'

'Why would she do that? It doesn't make sense.'

There's only one answer, but it means exposing myself to ridicule and rejection. Either way, it's now or never, and I can feel myself slipping over the edge.

'Lucie, I've grown to care for you deeply. Johanna recognized it and tried to sabotage our connection. I understand if you're not ready to hear this, but I want to be honest. I've fallen in love.' Our eyes meet. I search for a glimmer of hope, but Lucie remains inscrutable. 'If I wanted a photograph, it would be of you.'

Caught off guard, she shivers. But before she can say anything, her father's booming voice interrupts.

'First mate,' Arno shouts at me. 'Raise the anchor. Vancouver, here we come!'

***

Today, the usually rough waters in the Strait of Juan de Fuca are as still as a millpond. *Hoop* crosses the fixed but fluid boundary from the United States to Canada with only her bow wave marking the sea. She progresses along the wide waterway towards Victoria Island and our destination, the Empress Hotel.

With Lucie at the helm, I stand in the saloon, watching Arno calculate my wages as patiently as any sailor waiting to be paid off.

'It's going to be crazy busy when we land,' he says, handing over a wad of cash. 'I've been in touch with our friends over the radio. The press will be there, and a TV news channel needs an interview.'

'Then we'll be off to stay with family and friends,' says Anna. 'We've catching up to do and must take Mickie to hospital. What are your plans?'

I should be used to Anna's frankness. It still comes as a shock.

'Um… I don't have any… I haven't… er… made up my mind. Ah… I'll work something out,' I babble.

'You're welcome to stay on the boat for a few days and look after her,' says Arno. 'You'll be glad to be alone, no doubt. But then I'm going to move her to a dry dock and clean the keel.'

Swallowing this harsh dose of reality, I understand I should have heeded Lucie's advice and planned ahead.

'Not so glum, Plum,' Anna says. 'I have an idea.'

She sits me down and lays out a map. 'We have a cabin in the woods in the Okanagan Valley near Osoyoos. It's beautiful at this time of year. Stay for as long as you want. Our neighbours, old Mr and Mrs Kalpas, could use your help around their farm. If you want to go, I'll send a telegram to let them know.'

The maternal, ever-caring matriarch has thrown me a lifeline, and I grab it with both hands. This valley sounds ideal. All at once, half-formed dreams coalesce in my mind's eye. The idea of buying a typewriter and becoming a writer takes shape. Maybe I'll get hooked by the call of the wild and never return home. This opportunity could be the path with the heart I've been searching for. I've probably lost out with Lucie, but keeping a connection with her family leaves me with half a chance of seeing her again.

'Thank you, Anna!' My heart goes out to her in gratitude.

'It is a pleasure having you as first mate,' Arno says. 'I pride myself on judging character. You've always been honest and trustworthy.'

'I've always held your family's safety as paramount.'

'Hotel ahoy!' Mickie shouts from above.

**

As *Hoop* glides home, Johanna takes the helm to appear as if she's sailed from Panama single-handed, while Mickie is back in the rigging, waving her plastered wrist. And, putting me out of a job, Lucie stands on the prow, ready to throw the bow line to welcoming arms.

We approach the granite steps of the Empress Hotel—a Victorian testament to the far reaches of the British Empire—Johanna navigates to the dock with a surprising display of seamanship, taking her time to ensure a smooth and impressive arrival. Eager hands tie us to the mooring rings, and a gangplank deployed.

Count Arno Camaris, resplendent in his Tyrolean jacket, stands in the cockpit looking like Odysseus back from his travels. He gathers his wife and children around him, and they stand looking as imperial as the hotel while pictures are taken and the newsreel spins. Then, to whoops and cheers, they disembark to a crowd of admirers.

Feeling the warmth of a joyful reunion all around me, I feel an emotional let-down as I face the stark reality of being an outsider amid familiar faces. Turning off Dick and Harry, whom I suddenly resent, an anti-climax washes over me.

Slipping through the welcoming committee like a ghost at a feast, I head to the hotel, hoping to find sanctuary and a phone booth to call my sister. I'll have to call collect and tell her I've arrived. She can let my parents know. They'll be glad to hear I'm not coming back and causing problems at home.

A musty aroma lingers in the lobby of this once-grand establishment. The worn carpets and cracked leather armchairs are a curious blend of time and neglect.

While I search for the concierge, the place feels as lifeless as the stuffed grizzly bear standing in a corner and as cold as the tiger's stare hanging as a trophy on the wall. The only sound is the rattle of a teaspoon on a saucer as a waiter pours another cup of tea.

This oppressive atmosphere is an incongruous finale to a trip that started with high hopes and great expectations. Although I have only just arrived, I already want to leave.

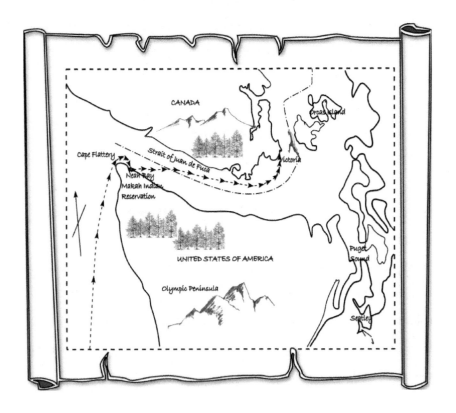

Chapter 16

Sheltering Walls

Staying the night on board with all the family gone, I feel I'm on the Marie Celeste, a ship found floating in the ocean with no crew aboard. By the galley sink, I spot a half-drunk cup of coffee, bite marks on a candy bar, and a dirty plate. Looking into previously unexplored lockers, I find emergency food supplies, batteries, sunscreen, and piles of Mickie's books jumbled away. Finding the sun-bleached hat and lone flip-flop strewn about, I feel a twinge of nostalgia, left behind as clues to a long passage concluded.

Stepping into the aft cabin, the girl's inner sanctum I visited rarely is ghostly quiet; the only sound is the gentle lapping of water. Even though they've gone, I shouldn't be here. I'm intruding on their private space. But the temptation's too strong to resist.

On Johanna's bunk lies the book containing the hidden pictures, now empty and disregarded. Next to it are Lucie's hand-me-down clothes swaying in a locker. The cabin is a microcosm of the mixed emotions swirling inside me. I take a last look and close the door.

In the saloon, Arno's last cryptic logbook entry, Wer das gold bewahrt! More Wagner, no doubt, sums up the cultural barrier I can't overcome. The laughter, shared sunsets, and camaraderie I thought were genuine are now illusions. Johanna's right: I was merely a deckhand with duties to perform.

The whole thing was an elaborate farce orchestrated by the *Klabautermann*, who knew about the smuggling and the risk we created for the family. Jerry ripping me off, Johanna ruining everything —all self-inflicted wounds made worse by the sting of betrayal.

Mickie is right, too. Magic exists. That's how life plays its trick. Finding Arno's bottle of schnapps, I drink a toast to secrets and lies and sink into oblivion.

***

Today, I let go of the stern line for one last time. Only now, I'm watching *Hoop* motor off into the distance with Arno at the helm, leaving me high, dry and on my own. With a reference letter from Arno, a map from Anna and a good luck card from Mickie, I take the ferry from Vancouver Island to the mainland. Leaving Pacific Central Station with a one-way ticket on a dusk-to-dawn Canada Greyhound, I set out on a rollercoaster ride to chase the moon to Osoyoos.

Leaving the city, the bus passes Chilliwack Mountain, heading up the Fraser Valley along the Crowsnest Highway. Even with the coach's gentle swaying and the engine's low hum, I cannot find a comfortable position. I drift in and out of a light sleep, catching glimpses through fluttering eyelids of a rugged landscape silhouetted against a sky filled with stars that stare back with cold indifference.

Dozing along with the ride, I reminisce about the trip. Having been cooped up together for so long, it feels a bit like leaving school—time to draft a report. Headmaster Arno is firm but fair, with an intriguing past. Matron Anna, with her compassionate heart, is my go-to person for a quick chat or a late-night cookie.

Passing over Jerry, the school bully, I continue with Mickie, who is good fun and carries no baggage. Darling Lucie, what an astonishing sailing companion. Why it had ended up wrong is a mystery. It's a busted flush, and I must get over it—no thanks to my nemesis Johanna, deadly as a scorpion. Then it's me. How do I fare at jumping through *Hoop*'s hoops? At least I wasn't expelled.

Just after dawn, the bus slows down to take a hairpin turn around Anarchist Mountain, revealing the breathtaking Okanagan Valley. It is a stunning panorama of rolling hills, lush vineyards, and glistening lakes stretching far, far away. In the distance, mountains with jagged peaks mark the boundary, their once wild and wooded slopes transformed into a patchwork of orchards and vineyards. The vision of a land of opportunity fills me with hope that out there is a path with a heart.

The bus drives down to a fertile plain with Osoyoos Lake, its centrepiece, a vast body of glacier water that stretches down the valley pitted with pioneer homesteads, hamlets and churches.

After driving past roadside stalls selling apricots, peaches, and plums, the Greyhound pulls up outside a Pay and Save store. The door swings open, letting in a waft of fresh air. I grab my rucksack and set foot onto the sidewalk.

Taking a deep breath, I step away from the bus. It feels Goldilocks warm, and while I orient myself with the map Anna drew, two flatbeds and a saloon car drive by in the morning rush. The town is a grid of two hundred modest dwellings on roads that radiate from a main street which slopes down to the waterfront, where a candy-striped building hints at a beach.

Heading to the gas station, I'm after a much-needed drink.

'Welcome to Joe's. What can I do for you today?'

'Hi there. I'm off the bus. I'll have a Coke, please.'

'Sure thing,' Joe, a middle-aged man in his late forties, comes across as though he's a fixture in the community. He wears a blue button-down shirt with the gas station logo embroidered on the chest. With hands soiled from work, he carries the sweet, heavy scent of motor oil that reminds me of Dick and Harry.

'What brings you to our little town, my hippie friend?'

I catch my reflection in the window. My hair is so long, it could be a bird's nest. My linen suit resembles crumpled parchment paper.

'I'm a friend of the Camaris family who has a place here.'

'Ain't seen them in a while.'

'They've been sailing around the world, and I was the engineer. I'm here to draft a book about the trip.'

'Well, you won't find much here to disturb you.'

'Where can I find a typewriter?'

'What! One of those loud, time-consuming things? You'd be better off with this.' He pulls a pencil from behind his ear. I laugh. 'I'll put the word out. You'll need something to keep you company.'

Showing him my map, he points me toward an old irrigation canal. From there, I take a meandering path through woods where the scent of vanilla from the ponderosa pines mixes with the fragrance of wildflowers abundant on the forest floor. When I spot a pine marten foraging in the treetops, and a melody of an unfamiliar bird song fills the air, this newfound wilderness casts a spell. I feel a kinship with all living beings and breathe in the pure essence of existence. Picking out the overgrown path, I clamber over brambles as though they're leading me home.

After weaving between the lattice of old tree trunks, I break out into the light, and there's the cabin. Nestled between woodland and pasture, it sits behind a post-and-rail fence. Made of logs, it is a childlike structure with a stone chimney stack and shuttered windows—a sanctuary where I can focus on living deliberately. The crooked steps lead up to a porch where I relax in an old armchair and gently rock back and forth till the mosquitoes come hunting. On entering, the screen door slams shut with a satisfying thwack, its loose mesh reverberating as if announcing a new arrival.

Aired and swept, the rustic cabin is one room with two doors leading off. In the kitchen area, next to a jug of wildflowers, someone's left bread, butter, milk, eggs and a jar of sauerkraut. I slap the table, announcing my occupancy. It's time to kick back and reinvent myself. Thoreau, your disciple has arrived!

***

When I set out to meet the neighbors in the morning there's a bright golden haze on the meadow. As I approach Jackpine Farm, a shiny black bullock looks up from a field of lush alfalfa. Restrained only by a flimsy post-and-rail fence, the powerful beast appears content to bask in the warm sun and chew the cud, unbothered by his minimal confinement. While I take in the picturesque scene, a sense of unease washes over me when the beast tilts its head, fixing me with an empty stare that seems unpredictable.

Knocking on the sturdy farmhouse door, I introduce myself and ask what the cow's called.

'Only a milker is given a name,' Lukas Kalpas replies in a thick Eastern European accent: 'Males have a different fate.'

Standing with his feet shoulder-width apart, he assesses me with eyes that have weathered life's storms. 'We are expecting you.'

His handshake is a test of strength, almost pulling me into the house before giving my shoulder a solid pat. I take his buzzcut as a sign of practicality, discipline, and toughness. A man not to cross.

'How is Arno?' I haven't seen him in two years.'

Eager to tell the tale, I begin recounting the adventure. 'Let me tell you about the skipper,' I depict him as a brave adventurer who navigated us through turbulent seas and challenging time to bring his family home. Lukas is captivated by the story. His eyes shine with wonder as he concentrates, his hands still on the armchair. He leans forward as the journey reaches its climax, eager to hear every word and uplifted by the hero's courage.

'I'm glad Arno got the trip out of his system,' he says at last. 'He talked about it for years. It was as though he needed to go in search of something he'd lost. I hope he found it.'

'Well, he was all made up when we got back. It was as though he'd made it back with the treasure.'

'Before war scattered us all to the wind, Arno's family was important. You can tell by the way he carries himself—he's a man born to rule. But in Europe, all our futures were torn away. Along with the rest of us, what he had was either stolen or burned, and nobody wanted to talk about it. We came here to escape and build cabins in the woods. Canada is God's country now! I'm glad Arno knows that.' He knocks on the scrubbed wooden table for luck while his wife Philomena clucks about, shooing the Devil from her door with quick, nervous gestures from her broomstick.

Sitting in their homely kitchen, Lukas tells me they rarely leave the valley. 'Once you've found paradise, you've got to stop looking.' Together, we men sip his 'bimber', an illegal brew of fruits, flowers, and roots with a musty aroma. I sense its powerful effects at once. Lukas notices and laughs. 'There's a joke around here that goes. How can you tell if you've had too much of Lukas' bimber? When you see two moonshines.'

Stumbling back to the cabin, I pass the bullock alone in the field. With his unflinching eyes, I can't help but draw a comparison to Jerry. Much like the bullock, he's an outlier, an isolated figure with the same potential for unpredictable actions.

***

With his children grown and gone, Lukas takes full advantage of Anna's telegram, saying I'd be willing to help. It's not even up for negotiation. You don't receive free sauerkraut as a welcome gift for nothing. Thinking helping around the farm would only involve taking my shirt off and chopping wood makes me as green as the grass in the field—my first job is to replace a filter at the bottom of the well.

'I dug it myself in forty-nine,' he says, crouching by the wellhead and lifting off the cover to an eighteen-foot shaft. 'There were only twenty houses in the neighbourhood then and no electricity. We had to draw water by hand, so when the power came, I put in a pump.'

Willing to try anything, I have been hoisted up a mast in a storm but, I can't shake this fear about being lowered down a well. When Lukas straps me into an old parachute harness. It's too late to worry.

'Digging a well is risky, as three around here go down eighty feet. Even though we newcomers spoke different languages, we all lent a hand to each other. Once you have water, you have life.'

Lukas inches me down into the darkness with our voices echoing off the water at the bottom. The cool, damp air shrouds me, and I feel the rough wood of the well-lining.

The water is twelve feet down, and I snake wrestle with a flexible pipe and replace the filter. Swinging on the rope in the dark like a marionette, it dawns on me that within a year, I've gone from stagehand to deckhand to farmhand, all essential jobs but hardly high status. I can understand why Johanna put the kibosh on me and Lucie. I'm no catch for a well-bred countess.

'Job done!' I shout up the shaft and feel the cranking handle rewinding me to the light.

On the way home, passing the alfalfa field, the bullock I've named Jerry in my head stands as a totem, a stark reminder of how he ripped me off, leaving me broke. Although I want to believe he betrayed me, he did warn me, quoting the soldier's rule: If it moves, salute it. If it doesn't, paint it. If no one is looking, steal it!

***

The smell of wood-smoke from the crackling barbecue, which we're using to grill and so preserve the Kalpas' bell pepper crop, catches in my hair. I spontaneously express gratitude for life's simple pleasures, and a burst of appreciation for the moment escapes my lips. Suddenly, I start whistling the tune from "Das Rheingold", picked up from Arno's serenading. I wonder if my hoard of gold is being here now. But the moment is short-lived.

'Keep your eye on the mountains,' Philomena sniffs the crispening air while pressing the green and red pepper flesh into Kilner jars. 'Once the snow comes, you can't get out. We have to be self-sufficient. We've no one to rely on but ourselves.'

Gazing up at the sentinels of the landscape, whose rugged contours form a natural barrier, protecting the valley from the outside world. I wonder if I'll survive the winter in Shangri-la.

Lukas packs the jars into a wooden crate, bedding them with straw. He lifts the hoard of winter supplies to carry them to the root cellar but stops short. 'It's good that you have found a job at the bakery,' he says, catching his breath. 'Matthias knows Arno better than anyone. They both lived in Vienna before the war.'

After a brief pause, he speaks in a loud voice that echoes across the yard, 'I'll need your help in the alfalfa field early Saturday morning. You'll have to get up with the birds. Don't be late.'

Nodding in agreement, I'm happy to help. I keep myself busy to avoid thinking about Lucie. Left alone for too long, I feel heartache, which, much like heartburn, is worse at night. I've been trying to channel my emotion into writing, but nothing comes when I sit down at the clunky typewriter Joe found. All I've done so far is scrape the ink out of the key slugs and clean up the casing with Lukas' bimber.

***

More than a little nervous, I arrive for work at Vienna Pastries at four in the morning. Matthias Lutz, baker and master pâtissier, is already hard at work in the back. His short, stocky figure moves around the bakery with a sense of purpose. He greets me with a friendly smile and hands me a glass of dry vermouth.

'This is how we start every day,' Raising his glass, he proposes a toast. 'To a good day's work!'

We clink glasses, and I take a sip of the dry liquid. It calms my nerves. I am ready to begin.

Matthias shows me the ropes, teaching me how to bake bread, buns, and rolls. At eight, Matthias' wife, Tudi, arrives to open the shop, her ready smile greeting the day's first customers. I retreat to the back to set about deep-frying doughnuts and filling them with jam. I'm soon lost in the rhythm of making eighty of them. My tasks are done by eleven, and I'm free to go.

***

When I arrive at the bakery this morning, Matthias is already hard at work weighing out the dough for loaves. His gaze lifts to meet mine, a slight frown creasing his forehead.

'The trouble with flour these days,' his voice, tinged with frustration, 'is that they steal its goodness before it gets here. They remove the bran, they remove the germ, and then they bleach what's left to make it white.'

I nod sympathetically, not knowing what he's talking about as we load up baking tins to let the dough rise.

'But this is great—bread's bread.' I say, weighing up the loaves.

Matthias gives me a wry smile. 'No! This bread is plain starch. In the old country, bread was a staple. You could live off it. You could buy three hundred kinds of loaves and a thousand different pastries.'

He pauses as if lost in memories. 'They were part of the way of life. He loved coming here to eat *Sachertorte*, his favourite chocolate cake, and talk about returning home to dig up old memories.'

'People here love your bread and pastries.'

'I do my best,' he says, casting a handful of flour on the wooden bench where he folds out the butter-rich croissant dough for pain aux raisins. When these pastries come out of the oven and are cool enough to eat, the frangipane in the flaky pastry layers flavours them perfectly. With every bite, you can taste the essence of Vienna.

'Only one a day with your coffee, Mick. Otherwise, you'll bankrupt me,' Matthias says, laughing as I drool.

We continue to work in companionable silence, the rhythmic movements of kneading and shaping dough almost meditative. Despite Matthias's concerns about the quality of the flour, I can't help but appreciate the beauty of the loaves we're creating, their golden crusts and pillowy interiors—a testament to the master baker.

***

Early in the morning, when the rest of the valley is asleep, the gentle rustle of sifted flour, the rhythmic tap of measuring cups, and the squeak of the oven door mean the town will have its daily bread. Amidst the warm, yeasty aroma that fills the air, where patience and care are the secret ingredients that transform basic ingredients into delicious bread, Matthias starts to unravel the enigma of Arno's past.

'Arno was a boy of ten when he joined the Hitler Youth after the Anschluss in 1938,' Matthias's voice carries over the rhythmic kneading of dough. 'He had no choice. But his family, were well-connected with ties to Goering so he was posted to an elite unit.'

Moving the trays of loaves from the proofing shelves to the oven, I remember myself at the same age as a Cub Scout, eager to fit in and follow the rules, proudly wearing the uniform.

'It was as if young Arno, was born to do it,' Matthias continues, his hands shaping the dough into rolls. 'He rose through the ranks and became a group leader reporting to the Gauleiter of Vienna. Even as the war turned sour, he stood firm in his allegiance.' Matthias's tone grows sombre. 'Then came the Russians, brutal and seeking revenge. Arno, penniless, manages to escape to Canada seeking refuge from war. And this is where we met—two refugee Austrians from different backgrounds enjoying chocolate cake.'

With oven cloths, I take out the loaves and empty the tins onto a rack. It's plain to me now why Arno is so complex.

'It's hard to imagine what he went through.'

Matthias nods solemnly, his expression grave. 'Yes, it was a dark time. But Arno is a survivor; he's built a new life here, and regardless of our differences, I call him a friend.'

'When did you leave? I'm now fascinated by the story as it develops. Matthias sighs as he recalls a distant memory.

'I used to work at a coffee shop in the fashionable district of Vienna, near the Imperial Palace.' His voice grows wistful. 'It was an elegant, cosy, popular place. The family who owned it offered me an apprenticeship as a pastry chef. It became home.' A shadow passes over Matthias's face. 'I didn't know they were Jewish until hateful slogans were painted outside, and customers stopped coming.' His expression darkens. 'The owners sent their son abroad, and since we were as close as brothers, I went with him—they were not so lucky.'

There's pain in his voice as he recalls the fear and uncertainty that gripped Vienna as the Nazis took control.

'Do you ever go back?'

Matthias shakes his head. 'I miss the *Ringstrasse* with its fine buildings, lush green spaces, and clip-clop of horse and carriage, but here the Gestapo can't knock on my door and drag me away.' He throws a handful of flour on the table and rolls out more pastry.

'Now go! Give my regards to Lukas.' He pats floury hands on his apron. 'And next week, less talk, more work.'

Wandering back to the cabin, I find it remarkable that two Austrians, one who fled the Nazis and the other who ran from the Russians, find common ground in chocolate cake.

***

A sudden jolt awakens me, and the moment my feet touch the floor, I am reminded of Lukas needing help with an early-morning chore. I dress and go outside. The air is cool as I walk across the dewy grass towards the alfalfa field. In the morning light he's erecting a tripod scaffold in the far corner. Below it lies the slaughtered carcass of 'Jerry'. It was the gunshot that woke me up.

'Come, help me with this block and tackle. We need to work fast before the flies come.'

We haul the dead beast up by its hind legs, and Lukas makes a quick incision, severing the carotid artery and jugular vein. The blood, now a river in the cow's coat, flows swiftly over the lifeless form and pools at the bottom of the pail. Its metallic scent, mingling with the earth's musk, binds us like butcher's glue.

As Lukas trudges back to the house, bucket in hand, his shoulders squared against the weight, I begin my task and dig a pit under the animal's head and lolling tongue. Left alone with the swinging sacrifice, I breathe in the bittersweet scent of life just gone and slap its rump goodbye. 'Bad luck, Jerry. You had it coming.'

The sun is rising as we butcher the carcass. Lukas slips his knife between the flesh and makes a precise incision, slicing down to the dewlap. Together, we grasp the hide and pull it hard, the sound of tearing flesh viscerally primitive. As the belly is exposed, the carcass's weight helps us flay the rest of the skin.

With the animal stripped of its hide, the exposed meat is intriguing and unsettling. Lukas guides the soft tissue bulge out of the body and coils of steaming entrails spill out, exposing the neatly packed secrets of life. After rummaging through the guts for the liver and kidneys, he reaches into the chest and slices through connective tissue to remove the heart—squeezing the blood out of it like a sponge.

'Back home, we have a saying: Don't sell the skin off a bear's back until you hold its heart.'

The morning air is heavy with the smell of death. The acrid aroma attracts the flies, but they're too late. All that's left is a blood-stained patch of soil, a mark for a life taken and the sustenance it will provide.

'Will you have some liver for breakfast?' Lukas asks as I wash the cleaver, knife and saw. 'You won't taste better. Alfalfa makes the juiciest meat.'

Not normally squeamish, I feel my stomach turn. 'No thanks. I'm good. I better clean myself up. Tomorrow perhaps.'

With a body charged with adrenaline and my sweat tasting of iron, I head to the lake to wash away the morning's work. Buck-naked, I plunge into the water. Its coolness envelops me and bathes away the remains of the slaughter. It is a cleansing, a baptism of sorts. As I float and gaze up at the sky, I feel relieved that Jerry will no longer haunt me from the empty field outside my window.

***

The thing about the land is that it smells. The sea doesn't. Walking back through the orchards beneath a clear early autumn sky, the air carries the sweet scent of ripening fruit. Picking an apple, I bite into its flesh. It's irresistible; no wonder the serpent found a willing victim. If I'm Adam and walking in Eden, where's Eve?

With my brain idling in neutral, a Wagnerian whistle leads me home, but it soon falls away as, outside the cabin, a car is parked.

'You're keeping the place tidy,' Lucie says as I walk in.

'Got to fill the evenings somehow,' I reply, surprised to see her but trying not to show it. 'What are you doing here?'

'I thought I'd come out and find out how you are getting on.' Her tone is confident but cautious, as if she's unsure how I will react to the surprise visit. While thinking of something to say, I nod like a buoy in choppy waters. In the course of being here I've grown accustomed to thinking of these sheltering walls as my own, I know they belong to Lucie by right.

'Look at this,' she says. 'Jerry sent us all a postcard from Mexico. There's a cryptic message on the back—Can you make sense of it?'

She hands me a picture of a smug-looking Jerry standing by a Striker 44 sports fishing boat and a dead marlin. Turning it over, it reads, 'Splash Stash Cash!' With a flick of the wrist, I toss the postcard onto the table in disgust. 'Tongue Twisting the knife,' I spit, shaking my head. Lucie looks clueless. I change the subject. 'How are your parents now it's all over?'

She walks over to the table, pulling dead stems from the vase. 'They're getting a divorce,' she says, *sotto voce* 'Papa's going back to live in Austria. He's obsessed with claiming what's ours by right. But Mama's not on board with his plan and was against him digging up the past in the first place. And now this.'

'Your father was restless, like he couldn't wait to be on his own,' I say, recalling their growing distance.

She glances at me. 'You should have said.' Her voice wavers, betraying a hint of underlying sadness.

'He dropped hints, but it wasn't my business.' My tone is harsh. 'If you remember, you weren't talking to me at the end.' There's an awkward silence as she takes the vase to the sink.

'What is Johanna up to these days?' I ask, keeping my tone casual. But in my mind, I can't help but think, Not that I care.

'Here's the thing. You won't believe it,' Lucie says, breezily talking over her shoulder while changing the water at the tap. 'She's on the radio lots, talking about the trip. How she loved every minute of it, doing the chores, mixing with diverse cultures, getting to know the locals, that kind of thing.'

'Lucky old Johanna'

Lucie misses my sarcasm. 'She's found her calling. Her passion for storytelling shines through. It's easy to imagine her hosting a show in the future. She's building up a following.'

'Gave up on being a porn star, then?'

Lucie ignores the crass remark and returns the vase to the table, surveying the stems as if working out how to arrange them.

'How's Mickie? Her arm must be mended by now.'

'Decided she's a lesbian and shaved her head,' Lucie states in a tone reminiscent of her mother's matter-of-factness. With sunlight streaming in low through the window, I spot her long eyelashes and feel that pang of longing, just as the flickers of lightning from the Sierra Madre mountains cracked my heart.

'Takes all sorts,' I reply, overwhelmed by a heavy weight of regret. I have an urge to run outside, to breathe fresh air and rid my heart of an ache for a love felt and never returned.

Lucie glances at me. 'You should have told me.' Her voice wavers, betraying a hint of sadness.

'What's become of *Hoop*?' I babble on. 'Have you sailed her since?'

'No! She's out of the water. Papa's repairing her keel.'

'Why; what was wrong with it?' The change of subject comes as a relief. Back on solid ground, we're talking about practical things. Lucie hesitates, glancing around as if afraid of being overheard; she leans closer and whispers. 'You can't tell anyone, okay? Promise me!'

'Promise,' I nod, intrigued.

'It's so exciting.'

'What's exciting?'

'It all makes sense now why Papa made the trip in the first place.'

'Lucie, you're babbling.'

'It's where he hid it.'

'Hid what?'

Lucie takes a deep breath. 'Papa, just eighteen in 1945, was in Vienna and part of the Gauleiter's inner circle, which he ordered to split up a stockpile of gold and hide it from the Russians.'

'Incredible, but what's it to do with *Hoop*?'

'Papa hid twenty gold bars in the grounds of our old family townhouse in Ringstrasse. He escaped just hours before the Russians took over the city. And get this: he's been plotting this crazy scheme to use *Hoop* to sneak the gold out of Europe to Canada to rebuild our family's fortune. It's unbelievable! None of us had a clue.'

As the revelation settles, I remember Arno's habit of inspecting the keel and his cryptic remark about waiting for someone to die—it all clicks. His return hinged on a grim truth: dead men tell no tales.

'You're telling me I was on a pirate ship all along?'

'More like a treasure ship returning our fortune.'

Conflicted by relative righteousness, I wonder if Arno's actions were more dishonest than Jerry's and mine. Either way, Lucie is out of my reach now.

'I'm sorry I was nasty to you, Plum.'

'Nothing but what a deckhand should expect from a wealthy countess.' I snap back. 'I got ideas above my station, that's all.'

Lucie sits at the scrubbed pine table, idly tracing the grain of the wood. 'It was all that nonsense about the photograph. Why shouldn't you have a picture of Johanna? She's more your sort.'

'What do you mean, my sort?' I demand, feeling annoyed.

'You know, sparky, vivacious,' she replies, startled by my outburst.

'Never wanted a choice,' I slump at the table. 'Not that it makes any difference now.'

'Don't say that. I don't know what came over me.' Lucie reaches out to touch my hand. 'I was jealous and lashed out.'

'Water under the bridge. We've all gone our separate ways. Memories fade.'

'Talking of memories.' she says. 'I've brought you a present,'. 'Something from the boat for you to remember us by.' She goes out to her car. The screen door slams, leaving me curious. It's probably a courtesy flag. Doubt it's a gold bar! Hope it's not the Elvis wig. God forbid her boyfriend didn't take to it, and I get it back as a joke.

Hearing Lucie's footsteps on the veranda, I sit up. She places a shoebox on the table. Without saying a word, she nods at it. Sensing her excitement, I reach out. Lucie leans forward, almost bouncing on her toes, as if she's willing me to find the surprise inside. Lifting the lid, I'm astonished to find Arno's Polaroid camera inside.

'Papa's got bored with it,' Lucie explains.

'Did he ever work out what was going on between us all?'

'No, he's all wrapped up in his own head. If you showed him the pictures, he wouldn't believe them.'

'Johanna showed them to you then?'

'Yes! Naughty, but not as you described.'

'How many?'

'Three.'

'There were ten.'

'She always kept the good stuff to herself.'

As if a dam has burst, uncontrolled laughter bubbles up between us. Tears stream down our faces at the absurdity of it all.

Then, all rinsed out, Lucie meets my gaze with a mischievous grin. 'It's dark in there,' she says, nodding towards the bedroom door. 'You'll need the flash if you want that souvenir.'

The End.

Available on Amazon, eBook, audiobook, paperback

Also available, the prequel

Long Lost Log: Diary of Virgin Sailor.

A Riveting Journey of Discovery!

 Here's what the critics say:

It's quite something—a wonderful read.

Afloat Magazine

Well written and genuinely funny.

Coach House Books

Fun, casual and simply enticing.

Book-blip.com

A rite of passage worth publishing.

Yachting Monthly

His vivacity is in the phrasing of extraordinary things.

Professor of Literature at Galway University

One of the best books I've read this year.

TikTok Influencer

Chapman Pincher is a natural penman. I was gripped.

Ed Maggs

It's a perfect gem of a book, and I don't like boats.

Irish Times

Acknowledgements

I want to express my gratitude to several individuals who have contributed to this project in significant ways:

Antony Farrell: Your constant encouragement and support have been invaluable.

Ian Smith: Your insightful copy editing has enhanced the quality of this work.

Charlie Doane: Your expert knowledge of nautical matters has added a depth of authenticity to this project.

Elaine Jones: Your never-ending proofreading efforts have ensured this project is as polished and error-free as possible.

Mathew George Martin. Your valuable insights helped tie up loose ends and bring the book to its conclusion.

To all of you, thank you for your assistance.

Michael Chapman Pincher

Feb 2024

Printed in Great Britain
by Amazon

43921418R00158